THE COMPLETE GUIDE TO CURRENCY TRADING & INVESTING

How to Earn High Rates of Return Safely and Take Control of Your Investments

By Jamaine Burrell

THE COMPLETE GUIDE TO CURRENCY
TRADING & INVESTING:
HOW TO EARN HIGH RATES OF RETURN SAFELY AND TAKE CONTROL OF YOUR INVESTMENTS

Copyright © 2007 by Atlantic Publishing Group, Inc.
1405 SW 6th Ave. • Ocala, Florida 34471 • 800-814-1132 • 352-622-1875–Fax
Web site: www.atlantic-pub.com • E-mail: sales@atlantic-pub.com
SAN Number: 268-1250

ISBN-13: 978-1-60138-119-4   ISBN-10: 1-60138-119-0

Library of Congress Cataloging-in-Publication Data

Burrell, Jamaine, 1958-
  The complete guide to currency trading & investing : earn high rates of return safely and take control of your investments / by Jamaine Burrell.
     p. cm.
  ISBN-13: 978-1-60138-119-4 (alk. paper)
  ISBN-10: 1-60138-119-0 (alk. paper)
  1. Foreign exchange market. 2. Foreign exchange futures. I. Title.

  HG3851.B87 2007
  332.4'5--dc22
                        2007019721

Printed on Recycled Paper

Printed in the United States

We recently lost our beloved pet "Bear," who was not only our best and dearest friend but also the "Vice President of Sunshine" here at Atlantic Publishing. He did not receive a salary but worked tirelessly 24 hours a day to please his parents. Bear was a rescue dog that turned around and showered myself, my wife Sherri, his grandparents Jean, Bob and Nancy and every person and animal he met (maybe not rabbits) with friendship and love. He made a lot of people smile every day.

We wanted you to know that a portion of the profits of this book will be donated to The Humane Society of the United States.

–Douglas & Sherri Brown

THE HUMANE SOCIETY
OF THE UNITED STATES ©

The human-animal bond is as old as human history. We cherish our animal companions for their unconditional affection and acceptance. We feel a thrill when we glimpse wild creatures in their natural habitat or in our own backyard.

Unfortunately, the human-animal bond has at times been weakened. Humans have exploited some animal species to the point of extinction.

The Humane Society of the United States makes a difference in the lives of animals here at home and worldwide. The HSUS is dedicated to creating a world where our relationship with animals is guided by compassion. We seek a truly humane society in which animals are respected for their intrinsic value, and where the human-animal bond is strong.

Want to help animals? We have plenty of suggestions. Adopt a pet from a local shelter, join The Humane Society and be a part of our work to help companion animals and wildlife. You will be funding our educational, legislative, investigative and outreach projects in the U.S. and across the globe.

Or perhaps you'd like to make a memorial donation in honor of a pet, friend or relative? You can through our Kindred Spirits program. And if you'd like to contribute in a more structured way, our Planned Giving Office has suggestions about estate planning, annuities, and even gifts of stock that avoid capital gains taxes.

Maybe you have land that you would like to preserve as a lasting habitat for wildlife. Our Wildlife Land Trust can help you. Perhaps the land you want to share is a backyard—that's enough. Our Urban Wildlife Sanctuary Program will show you how to create a habitat for your wild neighbors.

So you see, it's easy to help animals. And The HSUS is here to help.

The Humane Society of the United States
2100 L Street NW
Washington, DC 20037
202-452-1100
www.hsus.org

CONTENTS

ABOUT THE AUTHOR   275

KEY TO ABBREVIATIONS   277

INDEX   281

DEDICATION

———

In dedication to all the men and women who have lost their lives to a useless war for which they will never receive any benefit.

Many thanks to Shamia, Shamyia, Ciearah, Amonie, Daija, Kendrick, Shamar, Amira, Windaija and Johnesha

FOREWORD

By Mark Waggoner

P ortfolio management theory is simple financial economics: a diversified portfolio of uncorrelated asset classes can provide the highest returns with the least amount of risk.

Serious investors know they must diversify their portfolio. Most will turn to stocks, bonds, or real estate—all fine choices, but one must consciously seek out assets that do not move lockstep with each other. By its very nature, currency trading is inflation proof since it is not tied directly to the world's stock market, so that a portfolio will likely benefit despite conventional market fluctuations.

The art of currency trading is a sea of opportunity to the well informed. Being educated in how these markets work and how to use today's tools can transform you into a successful investor while actually reducing your overall risk. Information to navigate the liquid, easy-to-trade Forex or futures markets is abundantly available on the Internet in a plethora of trading platforms.

When I started investing in currency trading almost 20 years ago, we learned the basics by trial and error, and we made many mistakes! Even today, there are too few publications that provide basic information for novice traders. *The Complete Guide to Currency Trading & Investing* is now one of those few publications. Starting with this book, you can become a confident trader. Of course, any new form of investment strategy will take a serious commitment, but you will be greatly rewarded.

Mark Waggoner is the President of Excel Futures in Huntington Beach, California, and has been trading since 1990. He publishes a daily and weekly trade advisory: "The Trade Accord" and "The TrendTracker" respectively. Mr. Waggoner is frequently a guest on

Bloomberg Television and Radio and provides market commentary to Reuters and CNBC.

Mark L. Waggoner
President
Excel Futures, Inc.
16691 Gothard Street, Suite #L
Huntington Beach, CA. 92647
http://www.excelfutures.com
Toll Free: (888) 959-9955 / International: 01-714-843-9884

INTRODUCTION

———

There are some thrilling success stories in currency trading, and just as with any investment opportunity, there are risks. Novice currency traders need to understand that they must educate themselves so that their venture is a success.

This book provides readers with an understanding of currency trading and tells them how to avoid the risks involved. The art of currency trading depends on personality and a strong will to devote the time required. There is no one method of trading that will work for you or any other professional. This book helps you find the combination of moves that suits you.

Chapter One, "What is Currency Trading?," defines currency trading, the major currencies (the G8 currencies) and those currencies that are considered exotics. This chapter also outlines the financial entities that influence the currency market.

Chapter Two, "Central Banks," discusses those banks that have the most impact on currency markets and the most volume in currency trading. This discussion includes central banks of the major currency nations: the Federal Reserve Bank, the European Central Bank, the Bank of Japan, the Bank of England, the Swiss National Bank, the Bank of Canada, and the Reserve bank of Australia, as well as the central bank of the minor currency nation with the most trading volume, the Reserve bank of New Zealand. The governing body, important associated organizations, and programs are discussed for each central bank. This chapter also discusses the currency that each of these banks is responsible for and components of the particular nation's economy that affect the currency.

Chapter Three, "The Forex Market," defines the Forex market and the different Forex systems used by governments. This chapter differentiates the interbank market from the retail market, and it differentiates a Forex firm from a Forex dealer and a Forex broker. It specifies broker policies, suggests a method for broker selection, and discusses fraudulent brokers. It includes definitions of retail dealer platforms as well as online dealer and broker services. You will learn how to establish an online account and take advantage of other services available online. It also explains derivatives of the Forex market, including Spot, Forwards, Futures, Options, and Swaps trading.

Chapter Four, "The Language of Forex," delves into terms commonly used in the Forex market.

Chapter Five, "Fundamental Analysis," gives you the basics of currency trading. It outlines those economic, political, and social forces that drive a nation, particularly, supply and demand, interest rates, purchasing power, parity, economic indicators, balance of trade, and gross domestic product. It also defines those economic indicators that are important for the eight markets with the most trading volume.

Chapter Six, "Technical Analysis," goes into the technical components of currency trading to analyze charts and trends, support and resistance;

patterns used to determine trends; indicators and oscillators used to make market predictions, and the strategies for analysis.

Chapter Seven, "The Mechanics of Forex," examines money management, profit and loss, risk to reward and loss, and the psychology of trading. It also proposes a method of developing a generalized trading strategy.

Chapter Eight, "Trading Tactics," includes timing of the most influential markets and determining trading environments. It also provides some trading strategies that may be applied in these environments.

1

WHAT IS CURRENCY TRADING?

Currency trading is the trading of world currencies on the Foreign Exchange Market (Forex). The Forex market is used for simultaneously buying and selling currencies from countries around the world. This buying and selling activity is executed in pairs. The exchange, for example, may include an exchange of U.S. dollars (USD) for European euros (EUR). The Forex market is the largest financial trade market in the world. It is estimated to generate a volume of more than $1.9 trillion per day. The volume is estimated to triple that of stocks and other futures markets combined.

The Forex market includes spot trading as well as the derivative trading tools: futures, forwards, options, and swaps. The spot market is most commonly used in Forex because spot trading allows financial instruments to be traded at their current market price. Transactions are usually settled within two business days in contrast to other derivative markets where financial instruments are traded at some time in the future. More than 40 percent of all Forex trades are settled within two days and 80 percent all of Forex trades are settled within two weeks. Unlike other types of financial markets, the Forex spot market has no central physical location or exchange. It is purely an electronic trading process that revolves around a network of individuals, corporations, and banks. The Forex market operates 24 hours a day around the world.

MAJOR CURRENCIES

Currency trading may involve any currency backed by an existing nation. A listing of currencies used in Forex trading is shown in Appendix A. Of all the currencies in existence, the seven currencies listed in Table 1 represent the major Forex currency markets. Major Forex currencies are used in those nations with the highest trading volume. All other currencies are considered minor. Of all the world's currencies, the U.S. dollar is the cornerstone of the world's economy. Almost all foreign banks hold large reserves of U.S. dollars as security. One of the most crucial commodities in the world, oil, is paid for in U.S. dollars.

Each currency is represented by a three-letter symbol. In most currencies, the first two letters symbolize the nation and the last letter symbolizes the name of currency.

TABLE 1: MAJOR CURRENCY MARKETS		
Symbol	Currency	Nation
USD	Dollar	United States of America
EUR	Euro	European members
JPY	Yen	Japan
GBP	Pound	Great Britain
CHF	Franc	Switzerland (Confederation Helvetica)
CAD	Dollar	Canada
AUD	Dollar	Australia

The euro is an exception to the symbolism. Eleven European nations agreed in 1999 to remove their existing currencies from circulation and replace them with the euro. On January 1, 2002, the euro became the official currency of these nations and of a twelfth nation — Greece — which are known as the European Monetary Union (EMU). It includes the nations shown in Table 2:

TABLE 2: TWELVE NATIONS OF THE EUROPEAN MONETARY UNION (EMU)			
Nation	Old Currency	Old Symbol	New Symbol
Austria	Schilling	ATS	EUR
Belgium	Franc	BEF	EUR
Finland	Markka	FIM	EUR
France	Franc	FRF	EUR
Germany	Markka	DEM	EUR
Greece	Drachma	GRD	EUR
Ireland	Punt	IEP	EUR
Italy	Lira	ITL	EUR
Luxemburg	Franc	LUF	EUR
The Netherlands	Guilder	NLG	EUR
Portugal	Escudo	PTE	EUR
Spain	Peseta	ESP	EUR

In addition, the new currency was adapted by the following:

- The Vatican City

- The Principality of Andorra

- The Principality of Monaco

- The Republic of San Marion

- Any place that previously used one or more of the currencies that was used in the 12 euro nations as well as any territories, departments, collections, or possessions of those 12 European nations. These include the following:

• Europa Island	• French Guiana	• Guadeloupe
• Juan de Nova	• The Madeira Islands	• Martinique
• Mayotte	• Réunion	• Saint Martin

- Saint Pierre   • Miquelon   • The Azores

- The Balearic Islands • The Canary Islands

The euro is a currency used by some of the richest nations in the world. Used by more than 300 million people, the euro is considered a rival to the U.S. dollar. Many people expect that the euro will replace the U.S. dollar as the currency kept in reserve by the world.

THE G8

Another important group of nations in the currency market is the G8. The G8 is a group composed of the world's richest economies. The members of G8 include the nations shown in Table 3:

Table 3: G8 Member Nations		
Nation	**Currency**	**Country Code**
U.S.	Dollar	USD
Great Britain	Pound	GBP
Canada	Dollar	CAD
France	Euro	EUR
Germany	Euro	EUR
Italy	Euro	EUR
Japan	Yen	JPY
Russia	Ruble	RUB

World leaders of the G8 meet at least once a year for various reasons. Though many view these gatherings as simply photo opportunities for state heads, the meetings are used to influence currency levels. G8 meetings also provide insight into the global economic mood. When a nation is prospering or struggling, that nation's leaders use these meetings to discuss the nation's growth or current needs.

EXOTICS

Currencies of lesser-known countries are known as exotics. They offer trading opportunities but require research before investing with them. Actively traded exotics tend to be safer and offer tighter spreads, price execution, and price disclosure. The most actively traded exotics include the New Zealand dollar (NZD), the South African rand (ZAR) and the Singapore (SGD) dollar. Other exotics that should be mentioned include the Chinese yuan (CNY), Brazilian real (BRR), and South Korean won (KRW).

The Chinese yuan (or renminbi) is linked to the U.S. dollar, but the Chinese government does not allow the currency to float freely as does the United States and most other industrialized nations. It is expected that if the Chinese government does release hold of its currency, the yuan will become one of the major world currencies. The South African rand floats against other world currencies and is a major secondary currency in the market. The Brazilian real is only open to offshore counterparties but has floated since it was devalued in 1999. The South Korean won plays a major role in the Asian economic boom but is not easy to sell or buy.

CENTRAL BANKS' INFLUENCE

Each nation's government has some mechanism in place to control its supply of currency. Most countries have central or national banks that play a vital role in currency markets. The most influential central banks can lower and raise interest rates in an effort to control their nations' money supply. By lowering interest rates, a central bank makes it easier to borrow money, stimulating economic growth and consumption. In general, the market reacts favorably to lower interest rates and cautiously to rising interest rates. There are situations where rising interest rates attract money into the economy and thus, raise the value of a currency. For example, if the United States pays interest at one percent for deposits, Canada pays two percent, and Great Britain pays three percent, investors will put their money in the European economy to receive the most favorable return, boosting the value of the euro. The extent of the boost depends on market perception of how long the increases will actually last and the number of investors who take advantage of the opportunity. A listing of global central banks is provided in Appendix E.

OTHER FINANCIAL ENTITIES THAT INFLUENCE THE CURRENCY MARKET

Just about every country in the world has created some government agency to oversee trading securities and protect investors from fraud. That oversight is primarily reserved for futures and forwards markets, not the spot cash market used in Forex; however, there is movement toward exercising some types of controls over the Forex market in the United States and possibly other nations. Some of the important financial entities that influence the currency market in the United States are:

The International Monetary Fund

The International Monetary Fund (IMF) was founded in 1944 to prevent the market fluctuations that occurred before World War II. Each nation had devalued its currency to make its exports more competitive. The result was shattered economies and unrest. To avoid further destructive competition, the IMF was given the responsibility of ensuring that member nations implemented a stable exchange rate and a balance of payments. If a country suffers economic hardship, the IMF provides that country with a loan to avoid an upset of the global economy. These loans ,also called tranches, are funded by member nations, and they may be granted routinely or on an emergency basis.

The IMF is one of the most controversial institutions in politics. Though it has the responsibility for assisting nations, it is criticized for lending too much money, lending too little money, intervening too late, intervening too early, being too strict, being too lax, and subsidizing risky behavior. The most important aspect of an IMF intervention is that the nation in question is facing serious economic hardship.

The size of a tranche to any given country is determined by the size of the country's economy and its foreign reserves. Quotas are established for each nation. The six largest quotas are established for the United States, Great Britain, Japan, France, Germany, and Saudi Arabia. Each country is allowed to borrow up to 100 percent of its established quota. The first tranche acquired by a nation is usually provided with easy terms while successive tranches require more qualifications. As with any other creditor, the more funds the IMF loans to a nation the more control it requires of its investment. The IMF may impose higher interest rates and a more balanced deficit. The issue of control creates problems since a nation's economy is usually in shambles and the nation is on the verge of revolt by the time it seeks assistance from the IMF. The nation usually has no other alternative.

National Futures Association

The National Futures Association (NFA) is a self-regulated organization based in the United States. It provides regulatory programs, market integrity, and oversight to industry-wide futures and Forex markets. While the NFA establishes rules to govern the Forex market, the established rules are not laws. It is advised that participants in the Forex market deal only with companies that have some level of designation from the NFA. The NFA has been quite successful in convincing companies in the industry to register with them and thus abide by established rules. However, many companies have not become members of the organization. These non-member companies are considered to be unregulated, and their currencies should be avoided.

The NFA also maintains a list of companies that have been disciplined for sales practice fraud on their Web sites. Disciplined, in the terminology of the NFA, implies that a company was found to engage in deceptive telemarketing practices and to use deceptive promotional materials and, as a result, to be permanently barred from the market. A list of disciplined companies is provided in Appendix D.

Commodity Futures Trading Commission (CFTC)

The Commodity Futures Trading Commission (CFTC) monitors the activities of the NFA. The CFTC is a government organization that has jurisdiction over futures and Forex markets, but the CFTC does not establish rules for Forex trading. The CFTC gave that right to the NFA. The CFTC's regulatory authority is limited with respect to retail, over-the-counter Forex markets in the United States. No single entity has direct regulatory control of the Forex market, though the CFTC has begun to take on that role. The CFTC is granted authority to regulate the sale of retail over-the-counter Forex futures and options but only for regulated financial entities. Regulated entities include broker-dealers, FCMs, banks, and financial institutions. The CFTC also has the authority to abolish unregulated Forex entities, particularly unregulated FCMs.

Securities and Exchange Commission (SEC)

The Securities and Exchange Commission (SEC) exists to protect investors; maintain fair, efficient, orderly markets; and to facilitate the formation of capital to sustain economic growth. The SEC oversees securities, securities brokers and dealers, mutual funds, exchanges, and investment advisors. Some of the SEC's primary concerns are with maintaining fair dealing practices, promoting the disclosure of market-related information, and protecting market participants against fraud. In the United States the securities industry is governed by laws and rules that dictate that all investors, whether they be private individuals or large financial institutions, should have access to information about investments before buying them and for as long as they hold the investments. Therefore, the SEC requires that public firms disclose meaningful financial and other information to the public to provide a common knowledge base that investors may judge individually. The SEC prosecutes hundreds of civil enforcement actions against both companies and individuals each year for crimes such as insider trading, providing false or misleading information, and accounting fraud. The SEC continually reviews feedback from market participants, particularly investors, to find questionable market activity.

Foreign Regulatory Agencies

- Australian Securities and Investment Commission (ASIC) – An independent government body responsible for regulating financial markets, futures, securities, and corporations.

- Investment Dealers Association of Canada (IDAC) – A national self-regulatory member organization for the Canadian securities industry.

- Securities and Futures Commission of Hong Kong (SFC) – An independent non-governmental statutory body that has jurisdiction over securities and futures markets in the city of Hong Kong.

- Swiss Federal Banking Commission (SFBC) – An independent administrative authority of the Confederation that supervises particular areas of the Switzerland financial sector.

- Financial Service Authority of the United Kingdom (FSA) – A non-government, independent organization that has regulated the financial services industry in the United Kingdom since 2000.

- Bank for International Settlements (BIS) – An international organization that promotes international financial and monetary cooperation. The BIS serves as a bank for the central banks. The BIS is headquartered in Switzerland with two offices in Hong Kong and Mexico City.

Private Banks

Private banks play several roles in currency markets. They handle large trades for corporations, acting as the middleman for the transactions. Most large banks provide traders with money to trade or trade among themselves for a speculative profit.

Corporations

Larger, multi-national corporations are the big players in currency markets. Because global economies allow for the purchase and sale of commodities across foreign borders, the purchase or sale must be translated into the domestic currency and included in the company's balance sheet. Currency fluctuations could wipe out profits if the domestic currency is failing. Corporations may influence currency fluctuations by adding billions of dollars worth of currencies on the market for either sale or purchase. Corporations also engage in currency trading, and some corporations make as much money trading currencies as they do selling their products and services.

Currency Traders

Currency traders may be divided into two main groups: hedgers and speculators. Hedgers include companies and governments that buy or sell goods and services in foreign countries and must convert foreign currency into their own domestic currency. Hedgers trade currencies in an effort to protect their sales of goods and services from adverse currency fluctuations in foreign markets. A company located in the United Kingdom, for example, may sell GB pounds and buy U.S. dollars to hedge its profits from a fall in the pound. Hedging accounts for about five percent of the currency trade volume.

Speculators are those banks, home-based operators, and other investors who trade currencies for profit. Speculators may simultaneously buy one currency and sell another for profit. Speculation accounts for about 95 percent of the currency trade volume.

2

CENTRAL BANKS

Most central banks will intervene in foreign exchange matters to manipulate interest rates in an attempt to control inflation, one of the most feared conditions for economic policy makers. Lower interest rates tend to increase the affordability, and thus, availability of credit, which has the effect of putting more cash into the money supply. The extra cash is then available for goods and services so that as the demand for goods and services increases so do their prices, increasing inflation. A central bank's effort to raise interest rates during an inflationary period may have the effect of boosting the economy or it may further confirm that the nation is already in an inflationary state, which may cause market fear. Usually when a currency loses value because of inflation, that currency takes a loss in the currency market.

Some central banks, such as the U.S. Federal Reserve (Fed), the European Central Bank (ECB), the Bank of Japan (BOJ), the Bank of England (BOE), the Swiss National Bank (SNB), the Bank of Canada (BOC), the Reserve Bank of Australia (RBA) and the Reserve Bank of New Zealand (RBNZ), have a reputation for moving the market. Other central banks lack sound leadership and the financial strength necessary to influence the market. Traders need to gauge the general economic characteristics of the currencies used by those influential central banks to determine the currency's impact on market movements.

U.S. FEDERAL RESERVE BANK (OR FED)

The U.S. Congress established the Federal Reserve Bank, "the Fed," in 1913. It is independent from the federal government, except that it is subject to oversight by Congress which periodically reviews its activities. Decisions made by or on behalf of the Fed do not have to be ratified by the President or any other government entity. Congress also divided the United States into 12 districts and established a District Federal Reserve Bank in each of the districts. Further, the President has the responsibility of appointing a seven-member Board of Governors of the Fed, who oversee these district banks. Each member of the Board of Governors is appointed for a 14-year term. The relatively long-term appointment is intended to ensure stability and independence between presidents who are limited to two four-year terms in office. The president appoints the chairman of the Board for a term of four years, but the appointed term is renewable after the initial four years have expired.

Before the establishment of the Fed, the United States had no formal organization to study and implement monetary policies. The public had little faith in the banking system, and markets were unstable. The Fed is one central organization that promotes a sound banking system and a healthy economy. It serves as a banker to banks and the government, and it is the nation's money manger. It regulates financial institutions; promotes growth, employment, and price stability; moderates long-term interest rates; and issues all paper and coin currency. Though the U.S. Treasury actually produces the nation's currency, the Fed is responsible for the distribution of currency to financial institutions. (It is also the Fed that checks currency for wear and tear and removes damaged bills from circulation.)

Each of the Fed's district banks generates income from services provided to banks from foreign currencies held, from interest earned on government securities, and from interest on loans to depository institutions. Income is used to finance the day-to-day operations of the banks, and any excess income is deposited to the U.S. Treasury.

The Fed publishes the biannual Monetary Policy Report in February and July. It provides Federal Open Market Committee forecasts for inflation, unemployment, and gross domestic product (GDP) growth. The Fed also participates in the Humphrey-Hawkins testimony that follows soon after publication. During this testimony, the Fed chairman personally responds to questions posed by the Congress and banking committees with regard to information published in the Monetary Policy Report.

The Fed is governed by a mandate that establishes the long-term objective to create price stability and sustain economic growth. This is accomplish through monetary policies that limit inflation and unemployment to achieve balanced growth. The Fed has a reputation for reacting aggressively to economic changes and engaging in open market operations that provide for the purchase of government securities to manipulate interest rates and the federal funds rate either to reduce inflation or promote growth and consumption.

Federal Open Market Committee (FOMC)

The Fed is responsible for setting and implementing monetary policy through the Federal Open Market Committee (FOMC) which is responsible for establishing short-term interest rates used in the United States. Therefore, the Fed is the most watched bank in the world, not just by Congress, but by a multitude of entities around the globe. The president of the New York Federal Reserve Bank, presidents of four other district banks, and each of the seven members of the Federal Reserve's Board of Governors serves on the FOMC.

The New York Federal Reserve Bank has the responsibility of intervening in foreign exchange markets. The presidents of the four other district banks serve on the FOMC on a one-year rotating basis. The FOMC meets every month to review and discuss the economy and policy. All Fed bank presidents participate in policy-making discussions, and each board member is allowed one vote on establishing economic policy.

Federal Reserve Board (FRB)

The Fed's Federal Reserve Board (FRB) has the responsibility of supervising and regulating banks. The FRB monitors domestic banks, international banking facilities, foreign activities of foreign member banks, and U.S. activities of foreign banks. The FRB assists in ensuring that banks act in the best interest of the public by assisting in the development of federal consumer credit laws. Such laws include the Equal Credit Opportunity Act, the Truth in Savings Act, the Truth in Lending Act, and the Equal Credit Opportunity Act. The FRB also sets margin requirements for investors who limit the amount borrowed for the purchase of securities. The current requirement is set at 50 percent, which places a limit on a $5,000 investment to $10,000 worth of securities.

U.S. Treasury

While the Fed has the responsibility of implementing monetary policy, the U.S. Treasury handles fiscal policy, which includes determining the appropriate levels of government spending and taxation; therefore, it is the Treasury that actually determines dollar policy. The Treasury is also the government entity that assesses economic conditions and gives the Fed the authority and instruction to intervene in the foreign exchange market. The overall goal of both the Feds and the Treasury is to maintain a strong U.S. dollar.

The U.S. Dollar

The most liquid and most frequently traded currency pairs in the foreign exchange market include the U.S. dollar. These currency pairs include USD/JPY, USD/CHF, USD/CAN, EUR/USD, GBP/USD and AUD/USD. More than 90 percent of all currency trades involve the U.S. dollar, making it one of the most important currencies in foreign exchange. As a result, U.S. dollar fundamentals are the most important economic data that cause market movement.

Before the attack of September 11, 2001, the U.S. dollar was considered a safe haven for currencies since the risk of dollar instability was perceived as low within the trading community, particularly among global central banks. The United States was considered the safest and most developed market in the world, able to capitalize on its status and attract foreign investments at discounted rates of return. Seventy-six percent of global currency reserves were held in U.S. dollars. Since September 11, 2001, the United States has suffered increased uncertainty and has reduced its interest rates. Foreign investors and foreign central banks that were invested in U.S. assets cut back their U.S. holdings. At the same time, the euro gained precedence as a premier reserve currency and threat to the stability of the U.S. dollar. Central banks have begun to diversify their reserves and increase their euro holdings while decreasing their U.S. dollar holdings, making for one of the most closely watched trends in markets.

The USD Relationship to Gold

Historically the U.S. dollar and gold prices have had an inverse relationship where the value of the dollar would increase when gold prices decreased. Likewise, the dollar value would decrease if gold prices increased. Since gold is measured in dollars and it is considered a premier safe haven commodity (the ultimate form of money), uncertainty in

39

THE COMPLETE GUIDE TO CURRENCY TRADING & INVESTING

the United States has led many investors to invest in gold, thereby depreciating the value of the U.S. dollar.

Pegging the U.S. Dollar

Many currencies are pegged to the U.S. dollar because of its historic safe haven status and stability. Pegging insists that the U.S. government agree to maintain the dollar as a reserve currency by offering to buy or sell any amount of a foreign nation's domestic currency at an established peg rate. The pegged central bank, in return, agrees to hold U.S. dollars as a reserve currency in amounts at least equal to the amount of domestic currency in circulation. Central banks that are pegged to the U.S. dollar become large holders of U.S. dollars that they are free to manage. However, the trend in reserve diversification and toward more flexibility in exchange rates means that many central banks may have less need to peg with the U.S. dollar in the future.

The U.S. Dollar Index

The U.S. Dollar Index (USDX) is a gauge of the overall strength or weakness of the U.S. dollar. The index is calculated as a trade-weighted average of the currencies of six geometrically different markets. The USDX is also a futures contract traded on the New York Board of Trade. When news is reporting a weakness of the dollar or a decline in the trade weighted dollar, it is usually referring to this index. When the dollar is moving in one direction or another against a particular currency, a trade-weighted average may not show the same movement. Some central banks choose to base their decisions on the USDX rather than individual performances of currency pairs that include the U.S. dollar.

The USD Relationship to Stocks and Bonds

U.S. currency, like many other currencies, has a strong correlation with fixed income and equity markets. In general, when U.S. equity markets are rising, foreign investors seek to profit from U.S. markets. When U.S. equity markets fail, domestic investors attempt to sell their shares of local publicly traded firms so that they may take advantage of foreign investment opportunities. Fixed income markets that offer the highest yields are more likely to attract foreign investment dollars. Fluctuations and new developments that create movement in these markets require foreign exchange transactions. Any cross-border merger and acquisition (M&A) activities, particularly those that involve cash transactions, will affect the currencies of all markets involved since the acquiring party will need to buy and sell currency to fund the acquisition.

Differentials are closely examined when there are yield movements in government bonds and assets. The strength of the U.S. dollar and the yield on return of U.S. assets are related to the interest rate differential between U.S. treasuries and foreign bonds. The differential provides an indication of potential currency movements. Since the U.S. market is one of the largest global markets, investors pay close attention to the yields that are offered for assets. Investors are always seeking the largest possible yields. If U.S. yields increase and/or foreign yields decrease, investors would be more inclined to purchase U.S. assets, which would increase the strength of the U.S. dollar. On the other hand, if the U.S. yields decrease and/or foreign yields increase, investors may sell their U.S. assets and purchase foreign assets, sparking currency trading activity.

EUROPEAN CENTRAL BANK (ECB)

The European Central Bank (ECB) is the European equivalent of the U.S. Federal Reserve Bank. The ECB has the responsibility of determining monetary policy for the nations participating in the European Monetary Union (EMU). The ECB includes a Governing Council that consists of a six-member executive board and 12 governors of national banks. The six members of the executive board include the president and vice president of the ECB along with four other members. The executive board implements policies dictated by the Governing Council. The Council is the highest decision-making body of the ECB with the responsibility of determining the interest rate banks are charged for borrowing currency from the national banks. The interest rates established by the Council are as closely watched as the Fed's interest rates.

The six-member executive board is appointed by agreement with the 12 euro nations. The ECB also works with banks that are closely tied to Europe but are not using the euro currency. These nations include Great Britain, Sweden, and Demark. The combination of the 12 euro nations and the three non-euro nations is known as the Euro system. The ECB meets bi-weekly and has the power to change monetary policy during meetings by a majority vote. The president is given the deciding vote in the case of a tie. Typically, monetary policy changes are only implemented when an official press conference is scheduled to follow the meeting.

The primary goal of the EMU is to maintain price stability and promote growth. Monetary and fiscal policies are implemented to meet this goal. The ECB attempts to maintain an annual growth in its Harmonized Index of Consumer Prices (HICP) below 2 percent and to establish its measure of money supply (M3) to a growth of about 4.5 percent. The ECB uses open market operations and a minimum bid rate, known as the repo rate, to control monetary policy. Open market operations provide refinancing options and management of liquidity. The ECB minimum bid rate provides a target for monetary policy and establishes a level of borrowing for central banks that are members of the ECB.

The Maastricht Treaty

The EU developed a treaty on the European Union, known as the Maastricht Treaty, in 1992 to formulate preconditions for member nations wishing to join the EMU. Each member nation must meet strict requirements to assist the EU in achieving its goal of addressing inflation and deficits. Deviations may result in hefty fines against the offending nation. The conditions are as follows:

- Member nations must have a general government deficit that does not exceed three percent of the GDP. Although small, temporary excesses of the deficit will be permitted.

- Member nations must have an overall government debt to GDP ratio of not more than 60 percent. A higher ratio would be considered if such a ratio were shown to be decreasing sufficiently.

- Member nations must have a rate of inflation no more than 1.5 percent above of the average rate of inflation for the best-performing member nations. The average considers the 12-month rates that precede the assessment.

- In the preceding 12-month period, member nations must have had long-term interest rates not in excess of the average rates of low-inflation nations by more than two percent.

- In the preceding two years, member nations must have had exchange rates that fluctuated within margins of the exchange-rate mechanism.

The ECB is a different entity than the European System of Central Banks (ESCB). Both are independent institutions—independent of national governments and other institutions of the EU. Independence grants them the right to control monetary policy, per the Maastricht

Treaty. The treaty states that any member of the decision-making bodies cannot seek or take instruction from any other institution, government of a member state, or any other body.

The Euro

The establishment of the euro, which replaced all currencies of nations belonging to the EMU, made the EUR/USD cross currency the most liquid currency in the world. The movement of this cross currency is thought to gauge the economic health of both the United States and Europe. The euro is also known as the anti-dollar because movement of the EUR/USD currency pair has been dictated by dollar fundamentals in recent years. EUR/JPY and EUR/CHF are also very liquid currencies that are used to gauge the general health of the Japanese and Swiss economies. The EUR/USD and EUR/GBP cross currencies provide the greatest trade advantage since the pairs make orderly moves, have tight spreads, and rarely gap.

As a relatively new currency, the euro offers several unique risks that are uncharacteristic of other currencies. Likewise, the ECB has a short history, which makes it difficult for market participants to gauge how the bank will react to political and economic changes. The euro is currency for some of the largest European nations and nations of great importance to trading, such as France, Germany, Italy, and Spain. As a result, the euro is vulnerable to any political, social, or economic instability of these individual nations.

The Stability and Growth Pact

The ECB established a Stability and Growth Pact that outlined rules for member nations. These rules were severely breached during 2004. The ECB has yet to impose any type of restrictions on countries that breached the rules. A newly revised EU constitution has been rejected by some member nations. It provides for nations to escape penalty if they breach the established budget deficits. Legalizing breaches has led to a lack of confidence in the euro and the ECB. Some nations, such as Italy, have considered dropping the euro and returning to their original currency.

The Euro's Relationship to Stocks and Bonds

The 10-year German bund is considered the benchmark bond for the European community. Ten-year U.S. government bonds may be used to gauge the future of euro exchange rates, particularly exchange rates against the U.S. dollar. The differential between 10-year German bunds and 10-year U.S. government bonds is thought to provide the best indicator of euro movement. When bund rates exceed Treasury rates and the differential increases or spreads widen, the euro is looked on as a bullish market. If the differential decreases or the spread tightens, the market is perceived as a bear market.

The Euribor Rate

The euro interbank offer rate, also known as the Euribor rate, is a three-month fixed interest rate offered from one large bank to another on interbank terms of deposit. Traders compare the Euribor futures rate with the Eurodollar futures rate. Eurodollars are U.S. dollars deposited at foreign banks and other foreign financial institutions. When the spread between Eurodollars and Euribor futures widens in favor of the Euribor, investors tend to invest in European fixed assets. Merger and acquisition (M&A) activities have increased between the EU and the United States. Large M&A activities that involve large amounts of cash may have a significant short-term impact on EUR/ USD movements.

BANK OF JAPAN (BOJ)

Japan is the world's second largest economy. The Bank of Japan (BOJ) is the primary policy making body for the nation of Japan. The BOJ has operational independence from Japan's Ministry of Finance (MOF). As a result, the BOJ has complete control of monetary policies. However, the MOF has control of foreign exchange policy but directs the BOJ in executing all foreign exchange transactions. A nine-member board, known as the Policy Board, directs the BOJ. It includes the BOJ governor, two deputy governors, and six others who are selected based on their experiences or expertise in Japan's economics. However, the Japanese government often intervenes to keep the yen at favorable rates and to ensure that world exports remain competitive.

Over the past decade, Japan has experienced an economic crisis. In an attempt to develop new initiatives to stimulate growth, the BOJ holds monetary policy meetings twice a month, immediately followed by press releases and briefings. The BOJ also publishes a Monthly Report of Recent Economic and Financial Developments of new monetary or fiscal policies and any changes in sentiment of the BOJ. Since the MOF directs foreign exchange matters, comments from officials of the MOF are also closely watched.

Exports are the biggest contributor to the Japanese economy, and as a result the government favors a weakened yen. If the Japanese yen experiences a significant or fast-paced appreciation, the MOF and BOJ voice their concerns, but if there is no action by government, the market becomes immune to warnings. The history of intervention in Japan's currency markets has resulted in active manipulation of the Japanese yen through open market operations.

The Japanese Yen

Japan, with the largest GDP in Asia, is used to gauge the broader Asian strength. Japan has the most developed capital markets, which have historically attracted investors to Asia. Japan conducts significant trade with other Asian nations so that the economic and political problems that plague Japan negatively affect other countries. Likewise, political and economic problems of these other nations have an impact on Japan and movement of the yen.

The MOF and BOJ are important institutions that have the ability to move markets. The MOF is the director of foreign exchange interventions, and as a result comments from MOF officials provide significant information. The BOJ and MOF have a long history of entering foreign exchange markets when they are dissatisfied with the level of the Japanese yen. As an export driven economy, the Japanese government tends to favor a weaker Japanese yen. Japan's economy is closely tied to political officials and heads of large corporations. The MOF is in tune with political officials and corporate heads when it decides to intervene to depreciate a strong yen. The BOJ periodically receives information on large hedge fund positions from banks and will intervene when speculators are on the other side of the market.

There are three main factors behind MOF and BOJ interventions. First, intervention is sought when the yen moves by seven or more yen within a period of less than six weeks. Using USD/JPY as a reference, seven yen is equivalent to 700 pips. Secondly, interventions to depreciate a strong yen occurred above USD/JPY 115 level in only 11 percent of all BOJ interventions. Thirdly, the BOJ and MOF intervene when market participants are holding positions in the opposite direction to maximize the impact of intervention. Traders may gauge the position of market participants by looking at the positions held as advertised on the International Monetary Market (IMM) Web site at **www.cftc.gov**.

Toward the end of the Japanese fiscal year on March 31, Japanese cross currency pairs become very active. During this time, exporters convert their dollar-denominated assets to Japanese yen. Doing so helps Japanese banks rebuild their balance sheets to meet guidelines of the Financial Services Authority (FSA). These guidelines require that banks mark security holdings to market. In anticipation of the exporters' need to repatriate dollar assets, speculators may bid the yen higher in value in an attempt to take advantage of the increased inflow of currency. Following the end of the fiscal year, speculators close their positions and the Japanese yen tends to bias toward depreciation.

In addition to the active year-end crosses, time plays a role in day-to-day trading activities. Japanese traders usually take one-hour lunches between 10 p.m. and 11 p.m. EST, leaving junior and less experienced traders to handle their affairs. As a result, the Japanese yen may become volatile during this time since the market tends to become very liquid. With the exception of lunch hour, the Japanese market moves in a relatively orderly fashion unless some government statement, breaking news, or surprising economic data is released. However, there is some increased volatility during U.S. trading hours since U.S. traders actively trade both U.S. and Japanese positions.

BANK OF ENGLAND (BOE)

The Bank of England (BOE) was established in 1694 and is the oldest central bank in the world. The bank was initially established to provide government loans and then expanded to provide credit to the nation's banking system. In 1946, the bank was nationalized and operated strictly under government control. In 1997, the bank became free of this governmental control. As an independent entity, the BOE established the Monetary Policy Board, which operates similarly to the Fed's FOMC. The Monetary Policy Committee (MPC) consists of nine members who set monetary policy for the United Kingdom. The BOE has a responsibility of setting interest rates, managing the United Kingdom's foreign exchange and gold reserves, and managing the government's stock register.

The MPC is granted operational independence in establishing monetary policy for the United Kingdom. The committee consists of a governor, two deputy governors, two executive directors of the central bank, and four outside experts. Monetary policy is usually centered on achieving an inflation target, as set by the Treasury Chancellor. The target is determined by the value of the United Kingdom's retail price index – exclusive (RPI-X), which is the RPI exclusive of mortgage payments. The current target is 2.5 percent growth in RIP-X. The BOE may change interest rates to meet this target rate. The MPC holds monthly meetings, and market participants watch for announcements on monetary policy. They publish statements after every meeting plus a quarterly Inflation Report that details the MPC's predictions for growth and inflation over the next two years, as well as justification for any policy changes. The MPC also publishes a Quarterly Bulletin, which documents past monetary policy movements and provides an analysis of the international economic environment and its impact on the U.K. economy.

The British Pound

U.K. currency has three names that are used interchangeably – the British pound, sterling, and the cable. The British pound is one of the four most liquid currencies available to trade. Six percent of all currency trades involve the British pound as either the base or quote currency. The United Kingdom's highly developed capital markets are partly responsible for the high liquidity. GBP/USD is more liquid than EUR/GBP, but EUR/GBP is the leading gauge for U.K. economic strength because GBP/USD tends to be more sensitive to U.S. developments and EUR/GBP is a more purely fundamental trade since Europe is the United Kingdom's primary trade and investment partner. The United Kingdom's and Europe's currencies are interdependent such that movements in the EUR/GBP may affect movements in the GBP/USD and vice versa. Traders who trade U.K. pounds need to stay abreast of both currency pairs. The rate of EUR/GBP should always be exactly equal to EUR/USD ÷ GBP/USD. Even the smallest deviations from this ratio are exploited by market participants and quickly eliminated.

The GBP Relationship to Oil

Some of the largest energy companies in the world are located in the United Kingdom. Energy production represents ten percent of the United Kingdom's GDP. As a result, the British pound is positively correlated with energy pricing. Many member nations of the EU import oil from the United Kingdom and as oil prices increase, these nations have to purchase more U.K. pounds to pay for purchases. The United Kingdom's oil exporters then benefit from the increased earnings.

Speculation for U.K. Differentials

Many investors who seek investment opportunities outside of the United States choose to invest in the United Kingdom's highly developed markets. The pound has experienced some of the highest interest rates among developed nations. While Australia and New Zealand have offered higher rates of interest, these nations do not have well developed markets. Many investors who have existing positions or are interested in initiating new positions use the British pound to place long positions against U.S., Japanese, and Swiss currencies. The increase in carry trades has also increased demand for the British pound. Carry trades involve buying a higher yielding currency with the capital of a lower yielding currency or lending a currency with a higher yield and selling a lower yielding currency. Traders take positions in carry trades to gain the interest rate differential. However, a significant number of carry traders could increase the volatility of the British pound should the yield differential between the British pound and other currencies narrow.

The GBP Relationship to Stocks and Bonds

Market participants use interest differentials between U.K. gilts and other foreign bonds to gauge monetary flows. Interest rate differentials between U.K. gilts and U.S. Treasuries may be used to gauge GBP/USD flows. Interest rate differentials between U.K. gilts and German bunds may be used to gauge EUR/GBP flows. The German bund is often used as the basis for European yields. Investors use these differentials as indicators of the potential of capital flows or currency movements. Interest rate differentials may also be used to gauge the premium yield that U.K. fixed income assets are offering over U.S. and European fixed income assets or vice versa. The United Kingdom has a reputation for providing competitive yields while also providing safety of stability equivalent to that of the United States.

U.K. Bank Repo Rate

The bank repo rate is the interest rate used in monetary policy. While in most nations, market participants may gain insight into any bias toward rate changes by assessing comments from government officials; the BOE requires that members of the Monetary Policy Committee publish their voting records. Their individual accountability in monetary policy is used to assure market participants that comments represent the opinions of individual committee members, not the opinions of the BOE. Market participants must look elsewhere to find indications of potential rate movements of the BOE. Three-month futures contracts of the euro sterling reflect market expectations of the euro sterling interest rate three months into the future. These contracts also indicate U.K. interest rate changes, which affect fluctuations of the GBP/USD.

The U.K. currency market will be affected by any comments, speeches, or polls, particularly those made by the prime minister or Treasury Chancellor. Any indication of a decision to adopt the euro usually leads to downward pressure on the GBP while opposition to the adoption tends to boost the GBP because interest rates would have to decrease significantly to bring the GBP in line with the euro. An interest rate decrease would cause carry trade investors to close their positions or sell their British pounds. GBP/USD would decline because of uncertainty in euro adoptions. The United Kingdom and its current currency have performed well under the existing monetary authority. With 12 nations under one monetary authority, the EMU has not yet proven that it is capable of implementing a monetary policy suitable for its existing member nations. The EMU is experiencing many difficulties with its existing member nations breaching established criteria.

SWISS NATIONAL BANK (SNB)

The Swiss National Bank (SNB) is an independent central bank with a three-member board, known as the Governing Board of the SNB. The board has a chairman, vice chairman, and one other member who are responsible for determining monetary policy. All decisions are subject to a consensus vote. (The option with the most votes is the consensus.) The board meets once per quarter to review monetary policy, but decisions on monetary policy may be announced at any time. Unlike some other central banks, the SNB does not set a single interest rate target. Instead, a target range is established by the three-month Swiss LIBOR rate. Monetary targets are also important as indicators because they may provide insight on long-term inflation. The SNB focuses on the inflation target which is set at less than two percent per year, a measure based on the national consumer index. The SNB statement, "should inflation exceed two percent in the medium term, the SNB will tend to tighten its monetary stance," signifies that the SNB would loosen its monetary policies if inflation were perceived to exceed two percent. The SNB monitors exchange rates as well as rates of inflation since strength in the Swiss franc could lead to inflation. In particular, when global risk aversion causes capital flow into Switzerland to increase, the SNB, which generally favors a weak franc, will intervene to provide liquidity in the franc, involving SNB officials' commenting on the currency, liquidity, and the money supply.

THE SWISS FRANC

The unique characteristic of the Swiss franc is its safe haven status. The Swiss history of political neutrality and the banking system's policy of protecting the identity of its investors makes Switzerland the world's largest destination for offshore capital. The Swiss franc tends to move based on foreign economic and political events rather than domestic conditions. In times of global instability and uncertainty, investors invest in Switzerland. The goal of these investors is focused on retention of their investment dollars rather than appreciation of the investment amount. Funds will flow into Switzerland to take advantage of the safe haven status, causing the Swiss franc to appreciate regardless of whether monetary growth is achievable.

Members of the EU have been persistent in pressuring Switzerland to relax its practice of providing confidentiality in its banking system so that there is an increased transparency of its customer accounts. The EU attributes tax evasion and issues with prosecuting tax evaders to the confidentiality of the Swiss banking system. Switzerland has refused to comply with such requests because confidentiality is the core strength of its banking system. The EU has threatened to impose sanctions on Switzerland. Political entities in both the EU and Switzerland are negotiating for an equitable resolution.

The CHF Relationship to Gold

Switzerland is the fourth largest holder of gold in the world. Traditionally, the Swiss constitution mandated that at least 40 percent of the currency be backed by gold reserves, and although the Swiss constitution no longer includes this mandate, the positive correlation between gold and the Swiss franc remains in the neighborhood of 80 percent. If gold appreciates, the Swiss franc is most likely to appreciate in response. Since gold is considered the ultimate safe haven form of money, both the Swiss franc and gold benefit from any global or geographical uncertainty.

Carry Trading the Swiss Franc

Though Switzerland offers some of the lowest interest rates in the industrialized world, the Swiss franc is a popular choice for carry trades. Carry trades involve buying a currency with a higher interest rate and selling a currency with a lower interest rate to fund the purchase or lending a currency with a higher interest rate and borrowing a currency with a lower interest rate. Since the Swiss franc has one of the lowest interest rates, it is the often the chosen currency to be sold or borrowed in carry trades. The trader would need to sell Swiss francs against a higher yielding currency, usually accomplished with cross currency pairs such as GBP/CHF or AUD/CHF. These trades will then affect the EUR/CHF and USD/CHF currency pairs. To exit their carry trade positions, traders will need to re-purchase Swiss francs.

The interest rate differential between three-month euro Swiss futures and Eurodollar futures provides a gauge of Swiss and U.S. money flows.

The differential indicates how much more premium yield fixed income assets the Swiss are offering over U.S. fixed income assets or vice versa. The differential is of particular interest to carry traders who enter and exit the market based on positive interest rate differentials between international fixed income assets.

The Swiss Franc in M&A Activities

Switzerland's primary industry is banking and finance where merger and acquisition (M&A) activities are very common. M&A activities, particularly as they involve foreign entities, will affect the Swiss franc. A foreign company, for example, must buy Swiss francs and sell its own domestic currency to purchase a Swiss bank. Conversely, if a Swiss bank purchases a foreign company, the Swiss bank would need to sell Swiss francs and buy the domestic currency of the company's home nation. In either case, M&A activities that involve Swiss banks and companies will significantly affect the movement of the Swiss franc.

The Swiss Franc's Cross Currency Relationship

The EUR/CHF is the most commonly traded currency for traders who want to participate in Swiss markets. The USD/CHF is the least frequently traded currency pair because it offers a higher liquidity and volatility. However, day traders may favor the USD/CHF pair over EUR/CHF because it does offer such volatility. During times of global severe risk aversion, the USD/CHF develops a market of its own. The USD/CHF pair is really derived from EUR/USD and EUR/CHF since USD/CHF should be exactly equal to EUR/CHF ÷ EUR/USD. Market participants use EUR/USD and EUR/CHF currency pairs to price current levels of USD/CHF when the currency pair is illiquid and they consider the two currency pairs to be indicators for trading USD/CHF.

BANK OF CANADA (BOC)

The Bank of Canada (BOC) is focused on maintaining integrity and value of its currency. The BOC has a board responsible for setting monetary policy. The board is known as the Governing Council of the Bank of Canada. The seven-member council consists of a governor and six deputy governors. The BOC meets about eight times per year to discuss monetary policy changes. The BOC also releases a quarterly statement of monthly monetary policy updates.

The BOC ensures price stability by adhering to an inflation target agreed on with the Canadian Department of Finance. The inflation target is one percent to three percent. The perception of the BOC is that high inflation can be damaging to the nation's economy and low inflation equates to price stability, which equates to sustainable long-term growth of the economy. The BOC controls inflation with the use of short-term interest rates. If inflation exceeds the target, the bank implements tighter monetary controls. If on the other hand, inflation is below the target, the bank loosens monetary policy. The BOC has done well with keeping inflation within target.

The BOC changes monetary policies by manipulating the bank interest rate, which affects the exchange rate. These interest rate changes are not really designed to manipulate exchange rates but to control inflation. The BOC uses the bank rate and open market operations to implement its monetary policy. If currency appreciation reaches undesirable levels, the BOC increases interest rates to offset the rise. If currency depreciation reaches undesirable levels, the BOC raises rates.

Monetary Conditions Index

Monetary conditions are measured by the BOC with the use of its Monetary Conditions Index. The index is a weighted sum of change in the 90-day commercial paper interest rate and G10 trade weighted exchange rate. The weight is three to one for the commercial paper interest rate versus the G10 trade weighted exchange rate. The particular weight is chosen since it represents data from historical studies of the effect of changes in interest rates on the exchange rate. In short, a two percent increase in short-term interest rates is equivalent to six percent appreciation in the trade-weighted exchange rate.

The Canadian Dollar

Canada's economy is highly dependent on commodity. Canada is the world's fifth largest producer of gold and fourteenth largest producer of oil. The positive correlation between the Canadian dollar and commodity prices is near 60 percent. Increased commodity prices usually benefit Canada's domestic producers while also increasing their income from imports. However, strong Canadian commodity prices also have the effect of lessening outside demand for commodities in foreign nations, such as the United States.

The CAD Relationship with the United States

The United States imports 85 percent of Canadian exports. Canada has maintained a merchandise trade surplus with the United States since the 1980s. The account surplus has reached as high as $90 billion. Strong demand from the United States and strong energy prices have led to record high energy exports, making the Canadian economy sensitive to changes in the U.S. economy. As the U.S. economy grows, trades with Canada will increase to benefit the overall Canadian economy. However, a slowdown of the U.S. economy will create a reduction of import activities that will significantly hurt the Canadian economy.

Canada's proximity to the United States makes cross border merger and acquisition (M&A) activity very commonplace. As companies strive to gain globalization, these types of mergers lead to money flow between foreign nations that affects the currencies of both nations. The significant acquisition of Canadian energy companies has led to the United States' injecting millions of dollars into the Canadian economy, creating a strong growth in USD/CAD since U.S. companies have to sell U.S. dollars and purchase Canadian dollars to pay for such acquisitions.

Carry Trading the CAD

Interest rate differentials between Canadian cash rates and short-term interest rate yields in other nations provide an indication of potential money flows. The differentials indicate how much premium yield the Canadian dollar is offering for short-term fixed assets versus the premium yield for short-term fixed assets of other nations - of particular importance to carry traders who enter the market based on positive interest rate differentials between fixed income assets.

The Canadian dollar is a popular currency to use for carry trades with the United States. When Canada offers higher interest rates than the United States, the short USD/CAD carry trade increases in popularity because of the proximity of the two nations. However, if the United States increases rates or Canada reduces rates, the positive interest rate differential between the Canadian dollar and other currencies would narrow and speculators would react by exiting their carry trades, which would depreciate the Canadian dollar.

RESERVE BANK OF AUSTRALIA (RBA)

The Reserve Bank of Australia (RBA) is mandated to focus monetary and banking policies to ensure the stability of the Australian dollar, maintain full employment and achieve economic prosperity and welfare for the people. The RBA's monetary policy committee consists of a governor or chairman, a deputy governor or vice chairman, a secretary of the treasury, and six independent members who are appointed by the government of Australia. Changes in monetary policy are voted on based on the consensus of the committee. The RBA holds monthly meetings on the first Tuesday of the month, except for January, to discuss potential changes in monetary policy. Following these meetings, the RBA issues a press release that outlines justification for any monetary policy changes. If no change is made, no press release is published. The RBA also publishes the Reserve Bulletin monthly. Semi-annual issues of this publication in May and November include a statement on the Conduct of Monetary Policy. Quarterly issues, published in February, May, August, and November, include the Quarterly Report on the Economy and Financial Markets. These publications provide market participants with insight on any potential monetary policy changes.

The government of Australia believes that the key to long-term sustainable growth is to control the level of inflation. As a result, the government has established an informal consumer price inflation target of two percent to three percent per year. The inflation target is expected to preserve the value of money, provide discipline in monetary policy decision-making and provide guidelines for the private sector relative to inflation expectations. The inflation target also increases the transparency of RBA activities. Market participants know that when inflation or expectations for inflation exceed the target level, the RBA is prepared to intervene to tighten monetary policy with rate hikes.

All Australian interest rates are influenced by the interest rates established for overnight loans in the money market. Monetary policy involves setting interest rates on these overnight loans. Changes in monetary policy affect the interest rate structure of Australian financial systems and also affect the sentiment of currencies, meaning that the behavior of borrowers and lenders in financial markets is affected by this monetary policy. The RBA establishes a cash rate, which is the target rate for open market operations. The cash rate is charged on overnight loans between financial entities, giving the cash rate a close relationship with money market interest rates. There is a strong correlation between interest rate differentials and currency movements.

The Australian Dollar

The AUD Relationship to Gold

The Australian dollar has a strong correlation with commodity prices, particularly gold prices. Correlations have been measured at about 80 percent. Australia is the world's third largest gold producer. Gold accounts for about $5 billion in exports each year. As a result, the Australian dollar benefits from commodity price increases. Likewise, it depreciates when commodity prices decrease. When commodity prices are high and the fear of inflation sets in, the RBA may consider increasing interest rates to curb inflation. However, gold prices tend to increase during times of global, economic, or political uncertainty. The RBA leaves Australia vulnerable to economic decline if they decide to raise interest rates under this condition since inflation is not necessarily the issue.

Carry Trading the AUD

Australia offers some of the highest interest rates of developing countries. The Australian dollar is a popular currency for carry trades since it offers fair liquid currency. The popularity of carry trades was estimated to assist in raising the Australian dollar by about 57 percent against the U.S. dollar in 2001. Carry trades offer investors high yields when equity investments are offering minimal returns. Carry trades, however, only last as long as the actual yield advantage exists. Should other central banks increase their interest rate and the positive rate differentials between Australia and other nations narrow, the AUD/USD could suffer from an over abundance of carry traders.

Interest rate differentials between Australian cash rates and short-term foreign interest rate yields provide an indication of potential money flows. The differentials indicate how much premium yield the Australian dollar is offering for short-term fixed assets versus the premium yield for short-term fixed assets of other nations. The yield is of particular importance to carry traders who enter the market based on positive interest rate differentials between fixed income assets.

Weather Conditions Affect the AUD

Since commodities account for the majority of Australian exports, the GDP is sensitive to weather conditions such as drought that may damage farming activities. Agriculture accounts for about three percent of the GDP. The RBA estimates that a decline in farming activities could directly reduce growth in the GDP by one percent. Drought also has a direct impact on other aspects of the economy. Companies that furnish supplies and services to agricultural producers and retailers in rural farming communities are also affected. Australian history has shown that the economy is able to recover strongly after a drought.

RESERVE BANK OF NEW ZEALAND

The Reserve Bank of New Zealand (RBNZ) is the central bank of New Zealand and has a Monetary Policy Committee of bank executives who are responsible for reviewing monetary policy on a weekly basis. Meetings are also held about every six weeks to decide on changes to monetary policy. The final decision for any rate changes lies with the RBNZ bank governor. The minister and bank governor establish current Policy Target Agreements in an attempt to maintain policy stability and avoid instability in interest rates, exchange rates, and output. Price stability involves maintaining the yearly Consumer Price Index (CPI) inflation at 1.5 percent. If the RBNZ fails to meet this target, the government has the authority to dismiss the bank governor, although this rarely happens. The authority to do so serves as an incentive to meet the inflation target.

The RBNZ implements monetary policy changes with the use of an official cash rate (OCR) and open market operations. The OCR is set by the RBNZ to be used to implement monetary policy. The RBNZ pays interest and receives deposits at 25 basis points below the OCR. They also lend overnight cash at 25 basis points above the OCR rate. The RBNZ is able to influence the interest rates offered to individuals and companies by controlling the cost of liquidity for commercial banks. The objective is to compete with and attract the customers of banks offering rates above and below the bounds of the overnight rate. It is anticipated that customers will choose the RBNZ because funds may be borrowed at a lower cost and the yields are higher. The OCR is reviewed and manipulated as appropriate to maintain the economic stability of the nation.

New Zealand open market operations are used to meet the cash target, which is the target amount of reserves held by registered banks. The current target is $20 million New Zealand dollars. The RBNZ forecasts daily fluctuation in the cash target and uses the forecast amount to determine the amount necessary to inject into or withdraw from reserves to meet the target.

New Zealand Treasury

The New Zealand Treasury provides the following objectives that may be used as guidelines for fiscal policy measures.

- Expenses should average around 35 percent of the GDP over

the horizon used to calculate contributions toward future New Zealand superannuation (NZS) costs. During the buildup of assets to meet future NZS costs, expenses plus contributions should be around 35 percent of the GDP. Over longer terms, expenses minus any withdrawals to meet NZS costs should be about 35 percent of the GDP.

- Revenues should be sufficient to meet the operating balance objective. The operating balance objective is to offer a robust, broad based tax system that raises revenue in a fair and efficient method.

- An operating surplus should be maintained that on average over the chosen economic cycle is sufficient to meet the requirements for contributions toward future NZS costs and consistent with debt objectives.

- A gross debt below 30 percent of the GDP on average should be maintained over the chosen economic cycle. Net debt excludes assets to meet future NZS costs. Net debt should be below 20 percent of the GDP on average over the chosen economic cycle.

- Net worth should be consistent with the operating balance objective through a build up of assets to meet future NZS costs.

The New Zealand Dollar

New Zealand is a trade-oriented nation, and Australia is New Zealand's biggest trading partner. New Zealand benefits from a strong Australian economy that provides for companies to increase their import activities. The boom in the Australian housing industry that began in the late 1990s has required increased imports of building supplies from New

Zealand. New Zealand has fared well from the increased export operations. Australian imports increased by 10 percent between 1999 and 2002. The two nation's currency pairs, NZD/USD and AUD/USD, are almost perfect images of each other, with correlations of the two currency pairs reaching as much as 97 percent.

The NZD Relationship to Commodities

Commodities represent more than 40 percent of New Zealand's exports, with a 50 percent correlation between the New Zealand dollar and commodity prices. As commodity prices increase, the New Zealand dollar appreciates. However, the correlation between commodity prices and the New Zealand dollar is not totally dependent on New Zealand's trade activities. The performance of the Australian economy is also highly correlated to commodity pricing. As a result, the correlation between the New Zealand dollar and the Australian dollar creates a commodity linked currency. As commodity prices increase, the Australian economy benefits, translating into increased trade activity, particularly with New Zealand.

Carry Trading the NZD

New Zealand offers some of the highest interest rates of industrialized countries, making it a prime candidate for carry trades. The popularity of carry trades has led to a rise in the New Zealand dollar, also making it sensitive to interest rate changes. Should the United States increase interest rates, for example, New Zealand would have to offer competitive interest rates to prevent speculators from reversing their carry trade positions.

Interest rate differentials between the cash rate of the New Zealand dollar and the short-term interest rate yields of other industrialized nations provide good indicators of the potential for money flows. The differentials indicate how much premium yield NZD short-term fixed income assets offer versus foreign short-term fixed income assets. Carry traders enter and exit the market based on the positive interest rate differential between global fixed income assets.

Weather Conditions Affect the NZD

Like Australia, New Zealand's economy is vulnerable to drought and other bad weather conditions. The economy is export driven based on commodities that it exports. Drought is very common in Australia, which is New Zealand's largest trading partner. In addition, droughts have a history of damaging New Zealand's farming activities. (In 1998, droughts cost the country over $50 million.) Droughts have cost Australia up to one percent in GDP, which equates to a negative impact on the New Zealand trading activities and economy.

Migration Affects the NZD

New Zealand has a relatively small population and any increase in migration into the country will have a significant impact on the economy. Even small increases in migration are significant to the performance of the economy since a growing population increases the demand for goods and services.

3

THE FOREX MARKET

The Forex market has expanded over the years because of an increase in global trade and foreign investment coupled with the constant fluctuation of the dollar against other global currencies. Investors have been capable of realizing profits from the Forex market when other markets have become unstable. The Forex market offers advantages in trading that contribute to the stability of profit potential.

The Forex market is composed of a global network of currency dealers, primarily commaercial banks. These banks trade and communicate electronically or by telephone. Since there is no organized and physical exchange responsible for facilitating transactions, investors may engage in over-the-counter type transactions. As a result, the Forex market is similar to that of the National Association of Securities Dealers Automatic Quotation System (NASDAQ) market rather than the New York Stock Exchange (NYSE).

The spot trading of currency in Forex allows investors to interact directly with persons in the market who are responsible for currency pairing. Though most countries have some regulatory control over transactions in the Forex market, the market's governmental influence is relatively limited compared to other investment markets. As the market continues to grow and expand, it is expected that more governmental controls will be implemented. Currently, the market does not require investors to pay government fees, exchange fees, clearing fees, nor brokerage fees. Traditionally, the only way investors could access the foreign exchange market was through banks that engaged in commercial or investment transactions that included large amounts of currency. In 1971, exchange rates were allowed to float freely.

The foreign currency market has no correlation with the stock market. Currency traders buy and sell one currency against another, and the outlook for profit potential is determined by the relative value of one currency against another. In a bull market where the outlook is positive, a currency trader profits by buying currency in the positive market against other currencies. If, however, the outlook is not good, a bull market is created for other currencies and the currency trader profits by selling currency in the pessimistic market against other currencies. In either a bull market or bear market, opportunities exist for market trading. Spot trading and the lack of an exchange allows investors to trade for lot sizes that require investments of less than $1,000 in contrast to typical futures markets where the lot and contract sizes are determined by the exchange.

Anyone with a fast Internet access and knowledge of the currency market may trade currencies. Growth in the Forex market has been a direct result of the development of online trading platforms and the market's 24-hour availability. Currency traders may enter and exit the market at will, regardless of market conditions. The liquidity in the market is partly responsible for the Forex trading volume, in excess of $1.95 trillion dollars a day. Forex is the most liquid market in the world.

Big central banks that have historically manipulated market prices in other markets have been unsuccessful in manipulating market prices in Forex. The number of participants in the Forex market is so large that no single investor can control market price for an extended time. The size and nature of the Forex market also limits insider trading and other forms of fraud, which are less than that of any other financial market.

The Forex market provides for low transaction costs that may be considerably less than those in retail transactions. Under normal market conditions, the retail transaction cost, also known as the bid or ask spread, is typically less than 0.1 percent. Transaction costs for larger currency dealers may be as low as 0.7 percent. Both profit potential and loss potential are increased by the low margins and high leverage offered in the Forex market.

FOREIGN EXCHANGE SYSTEMS

Governments generally follow three different foreign exchange systems – free float, peg, and dirty float. A free float system lacks any form of government intervention or steering. The market is allowed to adjust prices according to supply and demand; this system provides officials with flexibility in establishing domestic policies and provides the smallest target for speculators. The peg system is also called currency board. Under this system, domestic currency rates are fixed to a single foreign currency or group of currencies. The peg system assists in providing stability and controlling inflation for smaller nations and developing economies; it limits flexibility of governments in establishing domestic economic policy and provides speculators with an easy target. The dirty float system incorporates both the free flow and peg systems. It differs from the free float system in that prices are not completely driven by market forces. Central banks may intervene in foreign exchange matters to influence currency prices. The dirty float system differs from the peg system in that currency is not legally pegged to any particular foreign exchange rate. The dirty float system is the most widely used system because it allows governments to intervene in foreign exchange matters in the best interest of a nation's economy. Intervention occurs when either an official regulatory agency or financial institution directly coerces the currency exchange rate by devaluating or revaluating a currency or by manipulating imports and exports. Intervention affects the market by causing erratic changes in exchange rates and market volatility. Intervention also provides an opportunity for traders to profit from the erratic market if proper stop-loss safeguards are put into place for trades.

Though the dirty float system is the most widely used, a peg system can be very attractive to smaller and developing nations. The peg system allows them to develop more credible monetary policies by fixing their currency to a more   stable and larger currency, thereby controlling inflation, reducing financial costs, having flexibility in lowering interest rates, and spurring economic growth. A viable peg system must have three primary components.

- An exchange rate anchored to either a single or multiple currencies.

- A long-term commitment to the monetary policy of the anchoring nation.

- Convertibility to the anchoring currency system.

These components provide the market with assurance that a domestic currency is backed by the anchoring currency of foreign reserves.

A disadvantage of peg systems is that they make easy targets for speculators in foreign exchange. The peg system may also prove to be unstable in the long run. Nations that attempt to strengthen their economies and monetary systems with the use of pegs limit the use of their own monetary and fiscal policy and become dangerously reliant on the anchoring foreign exchange policy.

INTERBANK VERSUS RETAIL FOREX

The Forex market can be divided into two tiers. The first tier is the interbank wholesale market. The second tier is the retail market. The interbank market is an informal network of brokers and dealers that trades with banks, central banks, and other large financial institutions, accounting for about two-thirds of the Forex trading volume. Trades in the interbank market are based on credit ratings and trading size, are in the hundreds of millions of dollars, and involve more than 200 international banks. Most Forex traders do not trade in the interbank because they fail to meet the credit and size requirements. Most traders trade in the retail Forex market, which is also called the client Forex market. Many speculators trade in the retail Forex market with an intermediary who then moves trades into the interbank market, a process that accounts for about 18 percent of the Forex trading volume.

The Forex market has no physical centralized location where trade information is collected and distributed. Forex traders must rely on the interbank market to get a sense of supply and demand trends in the market. However, most retail traders do not know about some currency trades until the trade is executed. In particular, large trades executed with the big players are quietly voice-brokered, meaning they are executed by telephone or other voice or electronic chat communication.

By the time such trade information is publicly disclosed, the participating banks have already anticipated the trade and adjusted their investments accordingly. Since Forex is an unregulated market, any two self-regulated agencies may engage in a trade and there is no requirement for either party to report trade information to a centralized exchange or any other institution. The specifics of the trade are known only to the participants, making them the only parties capable of engaging in a trade based on any newly established prices. Through the documented banking activity involved, banks get a clue of such trades and may respond accordingly. In this sense, banks have an advantage over the retail investor who is dependent on news feeds for trade information, which usually report these types of large trades after they have been completed and confirmed.

Banking activity like this, though not a dominating activity, plays a critical role in price movement and handicaps the retail trader.

Some of the big players in currency trading still handle their trades by telephone, simply because it keeps their activities private and secure. Even so, modern day trading includes the Internet and evolving technologies that provide retail investors with fast access to the Forex market. In fact, the Internet has been the primary cause of the shift in Forex markets from telephone and chat trading to online trading. The New York feds indicate that the use of electronic trading systems accounted for more than 54 percent of the total interbank spot trading in 2001, in contrast to less than 33 percent in 1998. Most electronic trades are handled through two primary electronic platforms, Reuters Dealing and Electronic Broking System (EBS). Reuters is a London based news organization, which was one of the first to establish an electronic platform to communicate with the global trading community. Reuters has a history of handling interbank trades for large traders. EBS is a UK based foreign exchange provider that was established in 1993. It is documented as having 2,000 traders on 750 global dealing floors. The advent of these two electronic platforms made traditional telephone communication obsolete. Most existing retail platforms have been modeled after the EBS electronic system.

FOREX FIRMS

Most large Forex firms trade in the interbank market with banks such as the Hong Kong and Shanghai Banking Corporation (HSBC), Deutsche Bank, or JP Morgan. When a trader uses one of the major global financial institutions, that trader is trading in the interbank market, which starts at $1 million. Each Forex firm has a market maker who maintains order and provides liquidity in the market through market trade pricing. In Forex market making, Forex firms receive feeds from outside providers such as EBS, Reuters, or the banks involved in the trades. Market makers review those outside feeds and establish pricing to offer to clients. Each Forex firm also has a market specialist who intervenes in market situations when there are temporary price disparities.

FOREX DEALERS

Forex dealers are responsible for making trading opportunities available to retail investors and providing an orderly market for retail investors. Forex dealers handle clearing, extend credit to investors, and provide a number of other back office operations. The role of the Forex dealer is a combination of market maker and market specialist in the equity market. When a retail trader views a quote, a Forex dealer is providing that quote. Firms that act as Forex dealers must register as Futures Commission Merchants (FCMs). The Commodity Futures Trading Community (CFTC), an independent entity of the U.S. government, provides a listing of Futures Commission Merchants (FCMs). This list is shown in Appendix B.

In the United States, FCMs are the market makers in retail Forex. The CFTC and National Futures Association (NFA) implement strict requirements for all FCMs. Requirements include adequate capitalization and specific provisions regarding ethics and anti-fraud. These requirements are similar to rules established for dealers and brokers in the securities market. Traders are cautioned against trading with Forex dealers who are not registered as a FCM.

Forex dealers do not trade in the interbank market, though some claim to do so. Retail traders do not have the credit rating or trading volume to trade in interbank so that Forex dealers provide traders an opportunity to trade in a limited subset of the larger interbank market. Retail traders are limited to accepting the price established by the dealer and the dealer's ability to trade on their behalf. Retail trade includes quotes that closely mirror those of interbank prices provided by Forex firms. However, the Forex dealer has no legally binding obligation to provide liquidity or an orderly market in extreme conditions, as Forex firms do, a fact documented in the account opening documents of most FCMs. Retail Forex traders are vulnerable under extreme market conditions because they deal with a single dealer, and if that specific dealer is unable to provide executable prices, the trader is at a loss. In addition, the leverage offered by most retail Forex dealers might eventually outpace actual trading activities. A crisis in liquidity occurs if the balance of buyers to sellers is tilted.

RETAIL PLATFORMS

Retail platforms may be either single market maker platforms or multiple market maker platforms. Single market maker platforms allow a trader to trade with a single counterparty on a single quote. Multi-market maker platforms allow a trader to choose with whom to trade and to choose from multiple quotes. All platforms are based on three types of trading mechanisms — Hub and Spoke, Request for Quote, and Click and Deal. Each of these trading mechanisms offers different advantages and disadvantages and traders should understand those differences.

Hub and Spoke Trading

Multi-market maker platforms may allow traders to engage in Hub and Spoke trading providing for multiple market makers to post bids and allowing participants to choose their own counterparty. All networked participants may post bids and offers while seeing bids and offers of other traders. The mechanisms of Hub and Spoke trading provide traders with the closest available view of an entire market, creating a transparency in trading that provides more depth and more competitive pricing since there is no price manipulation or trading desk. However, Hub and Spoke trading may quickly lead to a liquidity crisis if all the participants trade on one side and there is no taker for the other side of the trade. This scenario becomes crucial, for example, if a major crisis prompts traders to sell a particular currency. The currency will continue to drop until a buyer decides to buy.

The mechanism of Hub and Spoke trading is found in many institutional platforms such as Currenex and FxConnect. One version of Hub and Spoke trading allows traders to trade directly with one another on the platform, a version offered with Hotspotfx, CoesFX and GFTs Inter Trader Exchange that promises to be the future of retail Forex trading.

Request for Quote Trading

Traders may request quotes from a market maker using a platform that incorporates an instant messaging type feature. The request is usually for a currency pair and trade size. The response is a two-sided price quote. Request for Quote trading tends to favor the market maker since only the market maker has time to see the trade and positions before making a quote. A dealer may then adjust that price up or down before responding to a trader's request for a quote. Request for Quotes is an older trading mechanism still used and preferred in most trades in excess of $25 million.

Click and Deal Trading

Most Forex firms use the Click and Deal trading mechanism. The advent of the Internet makes the "what you click is what you get" (WYC/WYG) technology available to online computer users. Otherwise known as one-click dealing or executable streaming price feed, the Click and Deal mechanism provides live quotes that may be traded instantly. Most prices are streamed; that is, they are continually updated. The streaming data provide for an orderly and dependable market. Though there are established limits on the amount that may be traded on a price, the limit has proven to be more than sufficient to satisfy most retail traders. Click and deal trading limits the advantage that market makers have with Request for Quote trading. Market makers are required to post two-sided quotes, giving traders the option of trading on the quote or not trading on the quote. Traders have the advantage of seeing the quote price before revealing their intentions to the dealer, allowing a transparency in Click and Deal trading and providing a mechanism that is the complete opposite of Request for Quote trading. Instead of having the trader ask the market maker for a price or a given currency pair that the dealer may adjust, the trader sees the price before deciding whether to trade. Click and deal trading is the most common type of platform used in retail Forex.

FOREX BROKERS

Brokers in the Forex market exist to match buyers and sellers for a commission as brokers do in most markets. A listing of U.S. Forex brokers is shown in Appendix C. Brokers are not a big part of retail trade in the Forex market because investors in the retail Forex market deal directly with market makers or dealers. An Introductory Broker (IB) or FCM representative fulfills the role of a broker in retail trade.

Because there is no centralized location for Forex trading, interbank traders need to engage the services of a Forex broker to participate in market events. Most brokers may be found online; however, there are some brokers who use traditional voice and paper services, or both. The Forex market is generally an unregulated market, but many legitimate brokers are registered with certain regulatory agencies and should be capable of providing traders with suitable documentation. There are many safe and reputable Forex brokers to choose from, but traders must be careful to avoid illegitimate Off-Exchange Currency Dealers and other scams in the market.

BROKER POLICIES

Like all other business entities, currency brokers have contract agreements that outline the role of each party to the contract. Traders must be sure to read the fine print in a broker's contract and should pay particular attention to trading hours, available currency pairs, required transaction costs, rollover charges, margin requirements, margin interest, lot size requirements, and any requirement not fully understood.

Though most brokers operate on the same time clock used in the global Forex market, which is 5 p.m. EST Sunday through 4 p.m. EST Friday, traders must be sure to confirm trading hours with the chosen broker. Brokers should trade the seven major currency pairs, but some brokers will not risk trading certain cross currency pairs. Traders must be clear as to which currencies they will be capable of trading on a chosen platform. Transaction costs are applied to each trade and will offset any profit made from trades. Transaction costs are measured in pips, and the lower the number of pips the greater the profit. Traders may compare pip spreads across brokers to determine transaction costs, or they may use a less scientific form of comparison that involves examining the bid/ask spread of EUR/USD trades. This spread is from the most traded currency pair in the market. While a bid/ask spread of 2 pips is preferred, a bid/ask spread that does not exceed three or 4 pips is usually acceptable. Rollover charges, which are interests determined by the differential between currencies in a currency pair, increase as the differential between the two currencies increases. Traders must be sure to understand the broker's use of rollover charges and the exact time they are applied. Margin accounts earn interest that fluctuates with a particular country's market rate. Even when no trading activity is being

THE COMPLETE GUIDE TO CURRENCY TRADING & INVESTING

done, the account should continue to earn interest from the party that holds the account. Brokers establish their own lot as well as mini-lot sizes, when applicable. Lot sizes may vary from 1,000 to 100,000 units and mini-lots are offered at one-tenth of a lot. Brokers offer fractional unit sizes to allow traders to select any unit size of choice. Traders must ensure that they understand the lot sizes available under a broker's contract. As with any other contract, a contract with a currency broker should be carefully examined and understood.

FRAUDULENT BROKERS

The CFTC's Division of Enforcement has filed more than 80 cases of enforcement action against fraudulent financial companies since 2000. Hundreds of firms, owners, and employees have defrauded more than 25,000 customers of more than $300 million. Fraudulent firms have been known to offer bid/ask spreads in excess of 30 pips and require commissions for as much as $200 per trade. Many of the guilty parties have been prosecuted and sentenced; however, defrauded investors rarely recover the funds they lose. The CFTC identifies some of the most common practices that these frauds engage in as follows:

- Promising profit that is never delivered.

- Claiming that most customers make a profit when, in fact, most of their customers lose money.

- Claiming to be trading customers' funds when, in fact, they are stealing customers' funds.

- Advertising fake success stories, using fake customers.

- Providing customers with fake account statements that show false trading profits.

- Claiming long tenures in the business when, in fact, they have only been in business for a matter of months.

- Claiming to be a stable and solid firm and then disappearing with customers' funds and providing customers with no contact information.

BROKER SELECTION

Selecting a currency broker is a process that requires thought and work. Finding the appropriate broker who will assist in meeting an investor's needs is critical. The lack of a centralized exchange has created a pool of global broker platforms from which investors must choose. They should not simply choose the first broker that looks good or give in to high-pressure sales tactics. The process should be carefully completed as follows:

- Choose at least three potential prospects and complete a comparative analysis of the three. If the situation warrants, negotiate for the best possible deal.

- Check the links of disciplined financial firms listed on the NFA Web site to ensure that prospects have not been removed from the market. A current list can be found in Appendix D. NFA ID links may provide associated names and the types of violations engaged by defunct and fraudulent companies.

- Request references with up-to-date contact information.

- Check to see if the broker is regulated. The regulatory agency in the country where the broker is located should be capable of determining whether a particular broker is regulated.

- Engage in Forex discussion groups to seek information about chosen brokers. Be aware that brokers and their representatives also engage in discussion groups and may be the party providing answers to such inquires.

- Determine the brokers' requoting behavior. The nature of the decentralized market provides that all brokers will requote occasionally. Those who requote often, especially when the trader is winning, should be avoided. Some requoting in fast moving markets is expected, but requotes when traders have big wins is suspect.

- Review the paperwork of prospective brokers. A broker's documentation is usually available on the Internet. Compare the language of the documents for clarity, vagueness, and understandability.

- Request information from prospects and compare the responses of each prospect.

- Call any advertised numbers to ensure that they are valid numbers and to determine whether the listed contact is accessible and reliable.

- Compare account minimums, margins, pip spreads, account withdrawals, lot fees, and other factors that affect trade profits. Determine if fees and requirements are within market norms. Request hard copies of documents that specify these things.

- Take advantage of the paper trades and mini-accounts for prospective brokers to gauge the ease of use of their particular platform.

- Engage in discussion boards to gather other users' opinions of the chosen platforms.

INTRODUCTORY BROKER (IB)

An IB is a Forex broker who provides technical support and advice. A trader who seeks support and assistance in watching and executing trades may seek the services of an IB. Not a market maker as an FCM is, the IB must rely on an FCM for pricing and trade execution and refer all trade execution and floor operations to an FCM. The IB is more focused on the client and usually works with a single FCM, limiting the amount of market depth required of the client and the number of execution options offered to the client. IBs are prohibited from holding any type of funds on behalf of the client and must refer all funding matters to its chosen FCM.

ONLINE DEALER AND BROKER SERVICES

Traditionally, banks have manipulated the Forex market by guarding information, making the price discovery process difficult for outside investors, and ensuring that mistakes by outside investors were costly. Banks were responsible for keeping bid/ask spreads wide and transaction costs high. Because of advances in computer and Internet technology, retail traders may trade online with pricing and execution comparable to that used in the interbank market. The Internet has provided for the wide, instant dissemination of information among millions of people worldwide, leading to less costly trades, easier execution, and finer accuracy in currency pair pricing. A constant flow of orderly quotes is provided to traders, even during volatile periods.

Almost all Forex brokers provide an online platform for traders to conduct business. Most platforms are built to run under the MS Windows operating system and may include JAVA extensions or Flash animations. A good platform offers the following:

- Easy access to the order entry process.

- Bar charts of currency pairs being monitored.

- Easy access to a listing of currently held positions.

- An account summary that indicates current account balances, available margins, margins locked in active positions, and realized and unrealized profits and loss.

- A voice backup system that allows for traders to conduct business whenever the Internet is not accessible.

Online platforms include both online dealers and online frauds specifically classified as follows:

- **Bucket shops.** These platforms have no connection to the Forex market, except the association they fraudulently claim. Typically, bucket shops attempt to lure investors into engaging in currency futures and options rather than spot Forex trades, because it puts these companies in a position to swindle more money from unsuspecting investors.

- **Bookmakers.** These platforms exist to place bets on currency. Bookmakers are legitimate in some countries.

- **Retail market makers (RMMs).** These platforms form the majority of online dealer platforms. There is much variation in the organizational form of these platforms and the extent to which they make direct connections with the Forex market. Chosen platforms should be evaluated carefully.

- **Institutional market makers.** These platforms are very closely aligned with the Forex interbank market. Investors must be capable of meeting the account minimums required to trade on these platforms.

- **Institutional Forex.** This platform is the Intranet-based trading system of EBS, a consortium of nearly 200 banks that account for more than 50 percent of Forex bank trades. Participants must be banks.

ONLINE ACCOUNTS

A trader usually needs to complete four steps to open an online account with a Forex broker. Traders need to select the type of account, complete registration, activate an account, and confirm the account.

Online accounts also offer some disadvantages. Internet connections are subject to a network failure, and computer systems are subject to a power failure. While most trading platforms have some method to back up their power supply, the trader, particularly the home-based trader, should also have a backup. Even when both ends of an Internet connection have adequate power, an Internet connection could be lost for a number of other reasons. Any long-term or persistent disconnection problems should be addressed before trading under such a system. Traders should seek platforms that indicate whether a network connection is established and whether data streams are being collected real time. Viruses, hackers, and security threats are other disadvantages of online trading.

Opening an Online Account

Forex brokers offer both individual and corporate accounts. These account types may be further differentiated based on equity sizes. Investors may also open managed accounts, where the dealer buys and sells currency pairs and determines which trade sizes to transact on behalf of investors. Managed accounts provide investors with a Forex investment that is handled much like a mutual fund but with more risk potential. Traders may also open derivative Forex accounts, but inexperienced traders are encouraged to use spot market accounts because they are easiest to rollover. Most of the fraud in Forex is attributable to trading schemes in the futures and forwards markets.

Registration

Brokers establish their own requirements for account registration, but generally a trader needs to complete an application, complete a W-9 tax form, sign a risk disclosure form, and sign consent to conduct business electronically. These forms are usually available for download on the platform where the trader is registering.

Activation

Brokers will provide exact details of how to activate an account after registration is completed. Usually a credit card is validated for use or an initial deposit is required.

Confirmation

After an account is activated, a trader's identity is confirmed by the assignment of a username and password necessary to gain access to the account.

Complementary Services

Many platforms have integrated software products that provide investors with the ability to perform charting and technical analysis. A dealer platform may integrate a software package as part of an upgrade to their software, or they may partner with another firm that specializes only in the integrated product. The level of integration and thus compatibility of the integrated products vary from platform to platform. Dealer platforms may also offer bilingual platforms or accounting services to complement their trading services. Most retail platforms include news feeds to assist traders in their analyses of the market.

Charting Packages

Charting packages are standard with most Forex online accounts. A good charting package is necessary to represent historical price data visually, and it presents the trader with a tool to manipulate such data. Data may be displayed in time increments, by period, by currency pairs, and by a number of technical indicators. Traders need to investigate offered charting packages to determine the source of the data feeds used to produce the charts. Since Forex has no centralized market, data may be derived from any number of sources. No two feeds and their charts will be exactly the same, and no one feed is necessarily better than the other. Data feeds from EBS and Reuters may represent the true market better than other sources, but they are expensive. Most platforms use a single charting system and provide reference to others. Traders should invest in additional charting services and compare charts for more accurate data representation.

News Feeds

Advancements in electronic communication have provided quick access to information and news; however, many Web based news broadcasts tend to lag the currency market. Market indicators are usually broadcast after the information has spread within the trading community through other means. Since seconds can mean the difference between a loss and a profit, the late broadcast of news from news feeds may present a disadvantage for some traders. Event driven traders and those who trade on fundamentals should invest in higher level news feeds. Traders who primarily rely on news feeds to provide indicators should combine news feeds with television business news such as Bloomberg reports.

Help and Education

Many broker platforms offer educational and training services to first-time users. The platform should also include some form of customer service with clearly stated contact information or, as a minimum, a help directory and frequently asked questions (FAQ) menu. Platforms that offer news services or news feeds on their Web pages provide traders with information they may use in currency pairing and deciding positions.

Chat rooms are also provided on many platforms. While they offer an effective way of allowing traders to communicate with each other, they are not reliable. Traders should be cautious of unsolicited tips and advice from unknown persons and sources.

Paper Trading

Paper trading is an educational tool that many platforms provide to traders in the form of a demo account. Demos provide the trader with an opportunity to trade in a real time environment but with no real exchange of money. Demo trades exist only on paper. Traders get an opportunity to familiarize themselves with the particular platform and test trading strategies without assuming any risks. These types of demo accounts are offered for free and serve as a sort of hands-on advertisement and trial test of the platform.

Micro Accounts

Some dealers allow traders to establish mini accounts with as little as a $100 deposit. As with paper trading, these small accounts are useful to the novice trader in testing trading strategies and skills.

MANAGED ACCOUNTS

In a managed account, investors allow a particular firm or individual to trade on their behalf. Managed accounts provide investors with a tool to invest in the Forex market without having to contribute any hands-on involvement. For retail investors, in particular, a managed account offers the benefit of knowledge, experience, and resources from an investment manager without the investment restrictions that accompany a hedge fund and other types of investment opportunities.

Investors have the responsibility of choosing an appropriate firm that will manage and trade in their best interest. An investor must sign a standard account opening document and other documents that give the manager what is called limited discretion to trade on behalf of an investor and withdraw predetermined fees from the account, but it does not give the account manager full discretion to control all the funds in the account. Account managers trade through an FCM or bank but direct the client to open an account with the chosen firm. Managers may charge a fee not to exceed two percent. They may receive no more than a 20 percent return. Account managers are also required to disclose any other compensation derived from managed accounts.

In the United States, managed accounts are not required to be registered with the Securities and Exchange Commission (SEC). Further, if the account is used strictly in the Forex market, there is no requirement for the account manager to provide disclosure documents that include corporate or personal biographies, audited performances, trading strategies overview, risks, and other information that would assist an investor in making an informed and educated decision. On the other hand, if an investment account were used to trade futures, the account manager would be required under CFTC and NFA guidelines to present potential investors with disclosure documents. CFTC and NFA guidelines would also require that the account manager be registered as a Commodity Pool Operator (CPO), commodity trading advisor (CTA), or a registered investment advisor (RIA) who has educational and filing requirements.

DERIVATIVES

Derivatives are the spot trading, futures trading, forwards trading, and option and swap financial trading tools that interact with each other to move the market and affect pricing. Many inexperienced Forex traders tend to focus on the spot trading tool because of its simplicity and growing popularity. However, the mass focus on just one of the established trading tools limits an investor's ability to trade effectively.

Spot transactions are over-the-counter transactions handled outside an organized exchange. No one party can keep track of the spot activity since it allows investors to get in and out of the market at will; however, trades made through an organized exchange are managed, documented, and made available to investors. The CEM is an exchange that reports all outstanding positions for options, information that predicts the future of the market to other investors—an indication that cannot be acquired for spot transactions.

SPOT TRADING

Spot trading in the Forex market is called Forex. A Forex exchange of one currency for another is a simple simultaneous transaction that may be settled within two days, with the exception of Canadian transactions which may be settled within one day. The relative upfront simplicity of the spot Forex market has been partially responsible for boosting participation in the Forex market.

There are two parties to any contract, known as a short position and a long position. The party who is obligated to deliver a commodity holds the short position. The party who is obligated to receive the delivered commodity holds the long position. There are no restrictions or limitations in Forex trading as long as there are willing counterparts to a trade and liquidity in the currency pair being traded.

FORWARDS TRADING

A forwards trade is a trade in which the date of delivery for a commodity is established for some time in the future. Typically, a forward contract is engaged for one, two, three, six, or twelve months. Traders may use forwards to take advantage of interest rate differences between countries. For example, if the U.S. interest rate is established at five percent and the European interest rate is established at eight percent, traders may convert their U.S. dollars into euros to receive the higher interest paid by the European Central Bank (ECB).

In theory, traders may also buy U.S. dollars for some time in the future so that they lock in the favorable exchange. When the dollars are delivered at the later date, the trader will have more dollars left over, a theoretical situation because the price of a forward contract may be more expensive (or cheaper) than the current spot price of the currency. These types of differences in interest rates are usually factored into the cost of most forward contracts, as established by the market. In the theoretical situation above, a trader is not likely to have more dollars left over because the market would dictate that a more expensive forward contract be offered for euros because of the superior rate of return for the currency. The higher price attached to the forward contract is called a premium. A cheaper price is called a discount. In essence, the value of a forward is not determined by the market's anticipation of how much a currency is worth as compared to another currency, but the difference in interest rates offered by the two countries.

FUTURES TRADING

A futures trade is very similar to a forwards trade. A contract binds a buyer and seller in a trade of currency for a predetermined price at some predetermined time in the future. The difference between a futures and forward trade is that futures are traded on a regulated exchange and forwards are not. The Chicago Mercantile Exchange (CME) was the first to offer futures in 1972 when it was founded. A full range of futures is still available at the CME via the GlobeEx trading platform that makes futures available 24 hours per day.

Trades in the currency futures market incur a round-turn commission that may vary from broker to broker. Trades in the currency spot market incur a transaction charge per trade, calculated as the difference between the current bid price and the ask price. Margins are generally higher in the futures market than those required for the Forex spot market.

An investor must make a deposit on a futures contract. The deposit provides a margin or bond for the trade. If market events suggest that a currency will increase in value over the next year, a contract that locks in a lower price will have more worth. At the end of each business day, the difference between the price for a future and the market price of currency is established. The difference is then added or subtracted from the margin. Losses to the margin must be replenished for the trader to be able to hold a position in the market.

A futures contract precisely specifies the terms and conditions of a trade agreement. A futures contract should include the following components:

- Quality of the commodity

- Quantity of units

- Price per unit

- Date of delivery

- Method of delivery

The stipulated price is the agreed on price to be paid in the future on the date specified by the date of delivery.

Spot currency trades that cannot be settled within two business days are typically routed through an authorized commodity futures exchange. The International Monetary Market (IMM) is such an exchange. It is a division of the Chicago Mercantile Exchange (CME) that specializes in currency futures, stock index futures, interest-rate futures, and options on futures.

Contract Specifications

Table 4 shows some typical currencies traded through the IMM and the contract specifications defined by the CME. The contract size represents one contract requirement. Some brokers also offer mini-contracts that are usually one-tenth the size of a standard contract. The month's column indicates the months for delivery. The symbols H, M, U, and Z are acronyms used to represent March, June, September, and December, respectively. The hours specify the Chicago's local trading hours. The minimum fluctuation is the smallest monetary unit registered as one pip in price movement at the exchange. The minimum fluctuation is usually established as one-ten thousandth of the base currency.

Table 4: Futures Contract Specifications				
Contract	Trading Hours	Delivery Months	Contract Size	Minimum Fluctuation
Australian Dollar	7:20–2:00	H, M, U, Z	100,000 AUD	1 pt = $10.00
British Pound	7:20–2:00	H, M, U, Z	62,500 GBP	2 pts = $12.50
Canadian Dollar	7:20–2:00	H, M, U, Z	100,000 CAD	1 pt = $10.00
Eurodollar	7:20–2:00	H, M, U, Z	$62,500 EUR	1 pt = $25.00
Japanese Yen	7:20–2:00	H, M, U, Z	12,500,000 JPY	1 pt = $12.50
Mexican Peso	800–2:00	H, M, U, Z	500,000 MXN	2.5 pts = $12.50
Swiss Franc	7:20–2:00	H, M, U, Z	125,000 CHF	1 pt = $12.50

Commodity Trading Advisor (CTA)

A CTA is an expert in the field of trading commodities and futures contracts who provides investors with advice and strategies. Investors usually develop a one-on-one relationship with CTAs, a relationship that may provide investors with one of the most effective methods of learning about Forex trading. CTAs must be registered with the National Futures Association (NFA) and are required to pass a series three or a series seven examination.

OPTIONS TRADING

Options is a form of currency trading where an investor is given the option to buy a specific amount of currency at an established price on or before a specified date. Options differ from forwards and futures because options give investors the right to buy or not buy. Most investors who use options predict and rely on stability in currency exchange rates. Speculators, on the other hand, assume the risk in hopes of making a profit. Options are an effective and relatively cheap tool for hedging against fluctuations in foreign currency. The buyer locks into an exchange rate and then uses the option only if the situation warrants using it. Options require that a buyer pay a premium to purchase the option. If the buyer fails to exercise the option, the premium is forfeited. Premium prices are set by the market and adjusted according to how likely the market perceives that the option will be exercised. Some premiums are calculated as simply the difference between the current spot price and the future strike price. Other premiums use more complex calculations that account for market conditions and the deadline before the expiry date.

As with all currency exchanges, options require a seller (sometimes referred to as a writer) and a buyer. The right to buy currency is a call option. The right to sell currency is a put option. Options are both call and put. The price for which a buyer agrees to pay or sell currency is called the strike price or exercise price. The amount of currency that can be bought or sold under the option is called the principal. Options have a specific time limit before they expire (expiration date or expiry date). In the United States, a buyer may exercise a call option on any business day, including the expiry date. In the European market, a buyer may exercise a call option at any time, but no currency is delivered until the expiry date. In general, less than 20 percent of all options fail to be exercised by the expiry date.

Options may be bought, sold, and resold as market conditions warrant, and they may be bought on an exchange or over-the-counter. Most exchanges offer U.S. style options and standardize the options, setting a strike price, expiry date, and contract size. The CME is one of the major exchanges that offer standardized and customized currency options. The CME offers its options primarily in currencies with strong economies such as the U.S. dollar, Australian dollar, Canadian dollar, British pound, euro, yen, and the Mexican peso. Options bought over the counter are bought in interbank. Options offered in the interbank market are usually European style options where the terms of the contract are negotiated between the seller and buyer.

SWAPS

A swap is a combination of a spot trade and a forward trade. A swap agreement between two parties specifies a trade of currency on a specified date and an agreement to trade it back on another date. A swap provides investors with an alternative to borrowing foreign currency. An investor who needs liquidity in a currency may swap for the needed currency. Through a spot transaction, an investor may trade U.S. dollars for Japanese yen. Using a forward transaction, the investor also agrees to buy back the dollars in the future. The investor has use of the yen for business or other purposes in the process. Large corporations and other major players in the Forex market tend to be the most favorable to swaps. Individual investors rarely use them.

4

THE LANGUAGE OF FOREX

There are certain terms used in the Forex market that should be interpreted to mean the same thing by all parties involved in the trading process.

MAJOR AND MINOR CURRENCIES

Major currencies are the seven currencies that experience the highest trading volume. These currencies include the USD, EUR, JPY, GBP, CHF, CAD and AUD, as listed in Table 1. Six trades that involve major currencies account for about 90 percent of the total Forex trade. These six trades include USD/JPY, USD/CHF, USD/CAN, EUR/USD, GBP/USD and AUD/USD. All other currencies are considered minor. Of the minor currencies, the NZD, ZAR, and SGD are the three currencies that experience the most trade volume. It is difficult to determine the ranking of other minor currencies because of the many changes inherent in international trade agreements.

CURRENCY PAIRS

A Forex trade involves the simultaneous buying and selling of currencies.

The two currencies used in the trade are referred to as a currency pair, which is quoted as two currencies separated by a slash, for example, USD/GBP. The first currency is the base currency, which is the currency bought, and the second currency is the quote currency, which is being sold.

QUOTE CONVENTIONS

A Forex transaction may be quoted in either of the currencies included in the trade, but the quote must always have two sides. The exchange rate used in the Forex market may be expressed as follows:

Base Currency/Quote Currency   Bid Price/Ask Price

The following notation:

EUR/USD   1.2406/08

is an expression of such an exchange rate.

The base currency is always equal to one. The quote currency is equal to the amount necessary to purchase one unit of the base currency. The ratio of base currency to the quote currency may be expressed as a single value – the relationship between two currencies. For example, EUR/USD 1.2406 indicates that for every euro, a trader may receive 1.2406 U.S. dollars.

If the EUR/USD quote increases from 1.2406 to 1.2506, the change signifies that the euro is strengthening and the dollar is weakening. Likewise, if the quote decreases from 1.2406 to 1.2306, the change signifies that the dollar is strengthening and the euro is weakening. If the trend of the dollar shows that it is strengthening against the euro, it is more advantageous for a trader to buy USD/EUR. (This trade buys U.S. dollars and sells euros.) Likewise, if the market trend indicates a weakening of the dollar, a trader should sell USD/EUR. (This trade sells U.S. dollars and buys euros.)

In the currency market, market trends can be determined by examining currency pairs over time. The language of the market expands beyond generalizations such as, "The dollar is strong." Such generalizations are used to express historic trends and trading norms. The knowledgeable trader indicates the relative position of a currency in a currency pair. For example, "The dollar is strengthening against the euro."

The U.S. dollar is the basis of the global Forex market, and it is accepted universally as the basis for many other currencies typically expressed as the amount necessary to purchase one U.S. dollar, and thus, quote USD as the base currency. When USD is quoted as the base currency, the quote is in what is called European or indirect terms. When another currency is quoted as the base currency, specifically, the euro (EUR), the British pound (GBP), and the Australian dollar (AUD), the quote is in what is called American or direct terms.

Typically, when a bid price and ask price are being quoted, only the final two digits of the bid price are shown as follows:

EUR/USD   06/08

When the ask price is more than 100 pips above the bid price, three digits are displayed on the right hand side of the slash, for example EUR/CZK 32.2456/870. This occurrence indicates a weak quote currency.

BASE CURRENCY

The base currency in a currency pair is the first currency. The base currency indicates how much the base currency is worth as measured against the quote currency. USD is normally considered the base currency in the Forex market. Quotes are then expressed as a unit of one U.S. dollar. If, for example, a USD/JPY is equal to 1.582, one U.S. dollar is worth 1.582 Japanese yen.

QUOTE CURRENCY

The quote currency is the second currency in a currency pair. The quote currency is also referred to as the "pip" currency. Any unrealized loss or profit is expressed in the quote currency.

CROSS CURRENCY PAIRS

Cross currency, or cross rate, is a currency pair that does not include U.S. dollars or the euro. Cross currency pairs effectively equate to two separate currency pairs. A GBP/JPY trade, for example, is equivalent to buying a GBP/USD currency pair and selling a JPY/USD currency pair or buying a GBP/EUR currency pair and selling a JPY/EUR currency pair. As a result, cross currency pairs are likely to carry higher transaction costs than currency pairs that include the U.S. dollar or euro. Currency pairs that include the euro are called euro cross currency pairs. The three most traded cross rates include EUR/JPY, GBP/EUR and GBP/JPY.

Since the Forex market provides for any nation's currency to be traded against any other nation's currency, there are hundreds of currency pairs in the market. When a cross trade involves one of the more obscure nations, the pairing is called an exotic currency pair, which offers a higher risk of liquidity.

Price Interest Points (PIPs)

A pip, also referred to as a point, is the smallest unit of price expressed for any traded currency. In the United States, it is the cent. Typically, a currency pair is expressed with five significant digits, and most currency pairs equate to a decimal value with at least one significant figure preceding the decimal point (i.e., a currency pair must include at least one unit of currency). The price in a bid/ask price quote is used to establish the number of pips. As an example, a bid/ask quote is expressed as EUR/USD 1.2406/08. The price is quoted to four decimal places. As a result, one pip is 0.0001 or 1/100th of a cent. The difference between the bid and ask price is calculated as the absolute value of the two values as follows:

$$| \, 1.2406 - 1.2408 \, | = | -.0002|$$

$$= 0.0002$$

Since

$$1 \text{ pip} = 0.0001$$

Then

$$2 \text{ pips} = 0.0002$$

Likewise, if a bid/ask quote is expressed as USD/JPY 1.06/09, the price is quoted to two decimal places and a single pip is 0.01. The difference between the bid price and ask price is 3 pips.

The value of each pip is calculated by dividing the currency's smallest unit of price by the currency exchange rate. In the EUR/USD example above, if the currency exchange rate of the euro with the dollar is 0.88, the value of each pip is calculated as follows:

$$0.0001 + 0.88 = 0.000113$$

TICKS

A tick is the smallest interval of time that occurs with a trade. Ticks do not occur at uniform intervals of time. Trades on the most active currency pairs, such as EUR/USD or USD/JPY, during peak trading periods may result in multiple ticks during a one-second period. On the other hand, trades during non-active periods with minor cross pairs may result in only one tick every two or three hours.

Pips and ticks may be graphically mapped to scale with the x-axis representing ticks and the y-axis representing pips. Theses graphs may then be used to evaluate the market over time or within price restraints.

MARGIN ACCOUNT

A margin account is used to deposit money with a Forex broker to serve as a security deposit for trades. The minimum amount required to be deposited into a margin account varies from broker to broker, but usually ranges from as low as $100 to as high as $100,000. Each time a new trade is executed, a percentage of the margin account balance is allocated to the margin requirement for the trade. The amount allocated is dependent on the currency pair involved in the trade as well as the currency pair price and the number of units being traded. The number of units traded is referred to as the lot size, which is always as expressed as a unit of the base currency. Lot sizes are usually traded for 100,000 even units, but some brokers allow traders to trade in odd lot sizes that are a fraction of 100,000 units.

LEVERAGE

Leverage, also referred to as gearing, is the ratio of the amount invested in a trade and the margin required of the currency broker. Leverage is calculated as follows:

100 ÷ the margin percent required by the broker

Leverage varies from broker to broker and may range from 10:1 to 100:1. Leverage provides an opportunity for traders to control relatively large amounts of security with comparatively small amounts of capital. A $500,000 trade leveraged at 100:1 implies that traders need only have 1 percent of the trade value deposited in their broker's margin account.

Trade Value = $500,000

$$\text{Leverage} = 1{:}100 = 1 \div 100 = 0.01$$

$$= 0.01 \times 10$$

$$= 1\%$$

$$\text{Margin} = 1\% \text{ of } \$500,000$$

$$= 0.01 \times \$500,000$$

$$= \$5,000$$

The margin gives the trader $500,000 in buying power with a $5,000 deposit. Traders must realize that the volatility of the foreign exchange market ensures that in the same manner a $5,000 investment increases a trader's buying power to $500,000 and magnifies any profit on the increased amount, that same buying power may also magnify one's losses.

MARGIN CALL

A margin call is a notification from a broker to traders that their margin deposits have fallen below the required minimum because an open trade has moved against the traders. At this point, the traders may be required to deposit funds into their margin account to maintain the minimum requirement, or the margin account may be partially or totally liquidated when the available margin amount falls below the required minimum.

Some brokers may engage in a margin call before liquidation occurs while others may not. Some brokers give traders a two- to five-day window of opportunity to replenish their accounts. Traders must be sure to understand the terms of their margin accounts, monitor their account activity on a regular basis, and use stop-loss orders on open positions to limit such risks. Most online trading platforms automatically calculate profit and loss for open positions.

REQUOTES

Requotes occur when a trading platform fails to give a trader the quote that was presented and chosen on screen but offers a less favorable quote. Requotes can differ by as much as 10 pips. When markets are fast moving, some requoting is expected; however, requotes that occur often, and more importantly, those that occur when traders are winning, are suspect. Requoting is one of the major complaints against online dealers and brokers. With technological advances, requotes are less of a problem in stable markets. Traders who take a loss because of requotes do not have recourse because the broker is not going to absorb the loss. Traders are advised to monitor pricing on a particular platform and if requotes occur too often, choose an alternate platform. Traders should also look for platforms that offer straight-through processing (STP), which allows zero interaction between the times a trade is placed and a trade is accepted. This type of processing provides no room for dealers to manipulate quotes or make order mistakes.

BID AND ASK PRICE

The bid price of a trade is the price for which the market is prepared to buy a specific currency pair. Traders may sell the base currency at the bid price. The bid price is shown as the first price in a currency pair. The ask price, also referred to as the offer price, is the second price in a currency pair of a trade and indicates the price for which the market is prepared to sell a specific currency pair in Forex. Traders may buy the base currency at the ask price. In the quote USD/GBP 1.4536/42, the bid price is 1.4536, which means traders may sell one U.S. dollar for 1.4536 British pounds. Further, the ask price is 1.4542, which means traders may buy one U.S. dollar for 1.4542 British pounds.

BID/ASK SPREAD

The bid/ask spread is the difference between the bid price and the ask price. The bid and ask prices differ by only a small amount. The lower price is the bid price and the higher price is the ask price. The spread is expressed in pips and is a function of liquidity and market conditions. The spread on most major currency pairs is 3 pips and 5 pips on all other currency pairs. Currency dealers may express a bid/ask spread without the inclusion of what is called a "big figure quote." A big figure quote is the first few digits of the exchange rate. In the example USD/GBP 1.4536/1.4542, dealers may quote 36/42 without making reference to the first three digits.

The bid/ask spread is one of the aspects of trading that can be manipulated by brokers to produce more profit for the broker. Every broker receives commission on trades, even those brokers who claim to require "no commission." The broker's commission is usually tied to the bid/ask spread. The broker or the futures commission merchant (FCM) may not charge upfront fees, but may hide their fee in the spread by deliberately increasing the pips for the spread.

Spreads may widen and create volatility in market pricing under certain market conditions. When a central bank decision or monetary decision is made, an unpredicted market event occurs. Market conditions become volatile or illiquid; market prices become instable and volatile.

LOT

A lot is a standardized trading unit of $1,000 leveraged 100:1. A lot gives a trader controlling interest in $100,000 worth of the base currency. Lots have no time restraints or expiration periods since they may be automatically rolled over in trade.

MINI LOT

A mini lot is 1/10 of a standard lot. A mini lot is a standardized trading unit of $100 also leveraged 100:1. A mini lot gives a trader controlling interest in $10,000 worth of a base currency.

ORDERS

For an investor to hold a position on a trade, the investor must make an order for the trade. There are five types of orders that may be used to trade. These orders include market order, limit order, stop order, order cancels order, and stop-limit order.

MARKET ORDER

A market order is an order to buy and sell currency at the current market price. In the fast paced Forex market, a position to buy or sell may change before an order is carried out, or a position may change because a quote is incorrectly stated. As a result, a market order does not guarantee a quote price.

LIMIT ORDER

A limit order provides investors with protection on their orders. A limit order prevents an investor from having to buy or sell currency at a higher or lower price than quoted. A buy limit order dictates that currency can only be bought up to the limit established by the limit price. A sell limit order dictates that a currency be can sold at or above the limit price. Some currency brokers may charge more to execute a trade with a limit order than they would for a market order. A limit order that remains active until the end of the day is called a GFD or "good for the day" limit order. A currency dealer will automatically remove the order at the end of the day. A limit order that remains active until the trader cancels the order is called a GTC or a "good till canceled" limit order. Traders have the responsibility of monitoring and canceling the order because the trade dealer will not cancel the order if not instructed to do so.

STOP ORDER

A stop order occurs when a predetermined price automatically triggers a trade. When the predetermined price is reached, a stop order converts to a market order for either purchase or sale. Stop orders may not provide the best return in an unstable market because a brief fluctuation in the wrong direction may cause an automatic trade when, in fact, the overall trend of the market suggests that keeping the order active would be best. A stop order does not guarantee the price established when the stop order was converted to a market order. In a rapidly fluctuating market, the market maker may change positions. Traders must be sure to understand the established policy regarding stop orders.

ORDER CANCELS OTHERS (OCO)

An OCO order is a combination of two limit orders, two stop orders, or a limit order and a stop order. An OCO order allows two orders to be placed with price variables above and below the current market value. When one order is executed, the other order is removed automatically.

STOP-LIMIT ORDER

A stop-limit order is a combination of a stop order and a limit order. When a fast moving market threatens to cause a premature stop order, the trader may also place a limit order, which prevents a stop order from being converted to a market order and instead converts the stop order to a limit order. If the price then moves beyond the desired price, the limit order prevents the trade from being executed.

REGULATORS

The Forex market has no central global entity responsible for regulation. Each country has its own form of regulation. Some of the global regulation authorities include the following:

Country	Organization		Purpose
Australia	ASIC	Australian Securities and Investment Commission	
Canada	IDAC	Investment Dealers Association of Canada	A national self-regulated organization
Hong Kong	SFC	Securities and Futures Commission of Hong Kong	Has jurisdiction over leveraged foreign exchange trading in the city of Hong Kong?
Switzerland	SFBC	Swiss Federal Banking Commission	Supervises certain areas of the Swiss financial sector
United Kingdom	FSA	Financial Service Authority of the UK	An independent organization that was given authority to regulate the financial services industry by the Financial Services and Markets Act of 2000
United States	CFTC	Commodity Futures Trading Commission	A government agency with jurisdiction over futures and Forex markets
United States (continued)	NFA	National Futures Association	A non-government, self-regulated organization that issues rules for Forex and futures transactions

TRANSACTION COST

A transaction cost is the cost for a round-turn trade. A round-turn trade implies both the buy of trade and an offsetting sell or a sell of trade and an offsetting buy of trade of the same size in the same currency pair. Transaction costs are a characteristic of the bid/ask spread and calculated as the ask price minus the bid price. The transaction cost in USD/GBP 1.4536/1.4542 is 6 pips, calculated as follows:

$$1.4542 - 1.4536 = 0.0006$$

Since 1 pip = 0.0001, 6 pips = 0.0006

ROLLOVER

Rollover is the process of rolling an open trade settlement forward to another date. The rollover process incurs a cost based on the interest rate differential of the two currencies in the currency pair. When investors buy currency, they do not actually have the currency deposited into their bank accounts; they have it reset or rolled over. A rollover allows an investor to hold on to retail Forex position indefinitely.

The international trading day begins at 5 p.m., New York time (EST) when the market opens in Singapore. All retail Forex platforms automatically rollover open positions to the next settlement date. Rollovers take place at 5 p.m. The exact time of other rollovers is dependent on the trading platform, and each platform is different; however, most rollovers occur daily at 5 p.m. EST. If a trade is made at 5 a.m., London time, the trade will be rolled over at 5 p.m. EST and continue each day for as long as the position is open at 4:59 p.m. EST.

An investor's account may fluctuate because of payments required for interest differential. Positions that open at 5 p.m. EST incur a rollover cost, which is an interest payment that is either paid from or applied to the position, dependent on the margin level, currency pair, and the interest rate differential. If the position is closed by 5 p.m. on the next day, no rollover occurs and no interest is paid or applied to the position. A rollover allows investors to maintain their positions without being required to have the currency deposited into their accounts or to have their positions withdrawn from a trade prematurely.

If a trade's deadline is a weekend away, a trader has a three-day rollover. Interest is calculated as the sum of interest for three days and added or withdrawn from an account on Wednesday at 5 p. m. EST. The three-day rollover offsets trades that would occur on the weekend, had the market been open.

INTEREST RATE DIFFERENTIAL

Interest rate differential is the interest charged for rollover. The amount of interest charged is dependent on the currency being traded. Since a trader lends in one currency and borrows in another, the trader's account receives interest at one currency's rate and pays interest at another currency's interest rate. Interest rates are established from overnight lending rates set by London Interbank Offered Rates (LIBOR) or a derivative of such rates. It is for this reason that central banks are important to currency markets.

As an example, the prime interest rate established by the Federal Reserve Bank is two percent and that set by the Bank of England is four percent. Further, the respective LIBOR rates are the same. The spread between the GBP/USD trades is large. A trader would receive two percent of total amount traded so long as the margin remains at (at least) two percent. Interest is paid or charged by the Forex Capital Markers (FXCM) on a per lot basis. Any smaller position has to borrow money from the FXCM. Any interest earned is retained by the FXCM to compensate for the risk and service of lending the funds.

For most short-term Forex trades, the interest rate differential is of no consequence since most trades will exit the market before a rollover takes place. For longer-term positions, the interest rate and its precise application should be carefully weighed against the potential for profit or loss.

ARBITRAGE

Arbitrage is the purchase or sale of a currency while simultaneously taking the opposite position in a related market in an attempt to take advantage of small price differentials in the two different markets. Arbitrage is most prevalent when currency prices are out of sync with each other. There are many forms of arbitrage that involve multiple markets, currencies, options, and other derivatives. As a simplified example of a two-currency, two-market arbitrage, Bank X offers USD/EUR 200 and Bank Y offers USD/EUR 180. Making use of arbitrage, a trader buys 200 yen for 1 dollar at Bank X. The trader then sells those 200 yen for 1.11 dollars at Bank Y. If the exchange rates remain the same and the trader repeats the transaction, the trader profits as follows:

Bank X	Cost	Bank Y	Return	Profit
Purchase 200 yen	$1.00	Sell 200 yen	$1.11	11¢
Purchase 222 yen	$1.11	Sell 222 yen	$1.23	23¢
Purchase 246 yen	$1.23	Sell 246 yen	$1.37	37¢
Purchase 274 yen	$1.37	Sell 274 yen	$1.55	55¢
Purchase 305 yen	$1.55	Sell 305 yen	$1.69	69¢
Purchase 339 yen	$1.69	Sell 339 yen	$1.88	88¢
Purchase 376 yen	$1.88	Sell 376 yen	$2.09	$1.09

After seven transactions, the trader has more than doubled the $1 initial investment.

This type of two-currency arbitrage opportunity is not used in Forex, which involves two currencies in a single market. A specific trading strategy in Forex that uses three currencies is known as triangular arbitrage. Triangular arbitrage involves three currencies, discrepancies in their parity rates, and their correlation.

Intervention

The value of currency in any given country is volatile since it is affected by a number of economic and political conditions. The most notable conditions that affect the volatility of currency include interest rates, inflation, political stability, market orders, and international trade. Governments may influence the value of their currency by flooding the foreign exchange market with their domestic currency to lower the price or to buy a significant share of their domestic currency to raise the price. Government intervention in the foreign exchange market to influence pricing is known as central bank intervention. However, the volume and size of the Forex market prevents central bank intervention or any other factors from driving the market for a substantial time.

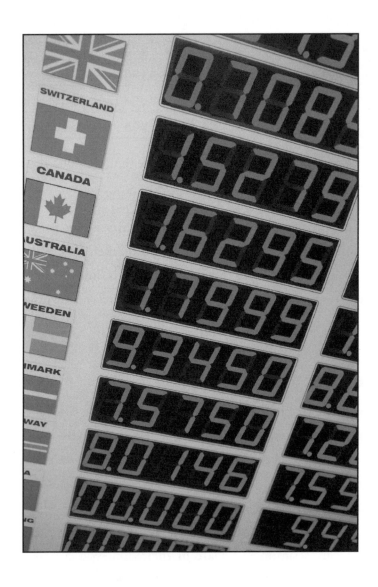

5

FUNDAMENTAL ANALYSIS

———

Fundamental analysis is the study of the core underlying elements that influence the economy of a particular commodity. It is a study that attempts to predict price action and market trend by analyzing those underlying elements within the framework of business activities and business cycles. Underlying elements include, but are not limited to, economic indicators, social factors, and government policy. Fundamental analyses provide the mechanism to describe how market conditions came to be and predict what time and price to expect in the future. While they provide an effective forecasting tool, they do not necessarily provide exact market prices. While such analyses provide a broad picture of the general health of the economy, traders need to develop their own method of translating the information to establish entry and exit points.

Fundamental analysis focuses on the economic, social, and political forces that drive a nation. Though there are theories as to how currencies should be valued, there are no established rules to guide the analysis. Traders must evaluate various macroeconomics such as inflation, budget deficits, trade deficits, unemployment, and growth rate indicators. In a fundamental analysis, traders need to understand how various reports, announcements, and events move markets. Even though market reaction is unpredictable, most skilled investors are capable of deducing how the market will react under certain circumstances. These traders rely on macroeconomic figures as well as government stability and its established policies. The impact of these various factors depends on the particular nation. The impact of an event in one nation must be compared against the impact of that event on other nations. Currency trading involves at least two currencies, and the weakening of one nation's economy does imply that all currency pairs that share the particular currency will trade lower. Pricing depends on how a weakening or strengthening economy affects that particular nation's situation and currency.

Currency movements are not mechanical reactions to events. Traders must understand how events, particularly unexpected events, affect the global trade market and one's position in the market. Information is the key to analyzing events. However, the importance of information is subjective. Various interpretations of the same information are responsible for creating volatility in the market. Market behavior, market psychology, predictions of fundamental changes, perceptions, and historical data are all factors in fundamental trading strategies. Fundamental analyses can be stressful for currency traders because this type of analysis does not provide specific entry and exit points, making it difficult for traders to control risks in leveraging techniques. The complexity is often the driving force that prompts some traders to engage in more technical analyses.

Fundamental analyses of the currency market include an examination of old news and fresh news. Old news is likely to be factored into Forex pricing while fresh news is expected to move markets. Fresh news is any unforeseen event that cannot possibly be factored into current pricing. Fresh news may also result from prescheduled economic events and other prescheduled events such as news conferences, interviews, and speeches. A single event may have the effect of moving the market and may also provide an excellent trading opportunity if properly evaluated. Fresh news will have the greatest impact on markets when such news is combined with a technical analysis of market conditions.

A fundamental trading strategy — news straddle — occurs when the nature of an event is unknown, but noticeable market reaction occurs in either direction as a result of the event. Traders place trades on both sides of an associated currency pair near the current price. They then apply their technical analysis to determine where to place orders, exits, and stops. Using this tactic captures a temporary volatility in the market as the market digests new information. Very experienced and educated traders are usually capable of making the most of this strategy.

SUPPLY AND DEMAND

The evaluation of economies required for fundamental analyses relies on an understanding of the supply and demand of currencies. The assumption is that the supply and demand of currencies is a result of economic processes that can be predicted and are observable in practice. The analysis involves an evaluation of the relationship between economic indicators and the evolution of exchange rates. A fundamental currency trading strategy includes a strategic assessment of the currency's tradability based on virtually any criteria, except price. Such criteria may include monetary policy, economic stability, and other factors fundamental to a nation's economy.

Economic indicators, such as trade balance, gross domestic product, and foreign investment, reflect the health of the economy and are responsible for a change in supply and demand. Currency pricing is a reflection of the balance of supply and demand while the strength of the economy and interest rates are the primary factors that affect supply and demand. Data that underlie most economic indicators are released at regular intervals by government or other sources. Of all the available data, interest rates, and foreign trade data are most closely analyzed.

RATES OF INTEREST

Any changes in interest rates have a direct impact on currency markets. The market typically reacts favorably in response to lowered interest rates as well as interest rates raised by fears. Some central banks have the authority to raise and lower interest rates in an effort to control their nation's money supply. Lowering rates makes it cheaper to borrow, stimulating economic growth and consumer consumption. Typically, when interest rates are raised, a nation's currency strengthens in relation to other currencies. The stock market, on the other hand, does not fare well when interest rates rise since many investors withdraw money from the stock market during this time, weakening a nation's currency. The trick for investors is to figure out which effect will prevail. In many instances, there is a consensus in the market as to what an interest move will result in based on a fundamental analysis of the consumer price index, producer price index, and the gross domestic product. The timing of interest rate's move is also important and is usually known in advance since these moves are normally implemented following regular meetings of central banks.

PURCHASING POWER PARITY (PPP)

PPP is a theory that establishes that the exchange rates between two currencies are in equilibrium when the purchasing power of the currency is the same in each nation. The theory implies that the exchange rate between two nations should be equal to the ratio of price levels for a fixed basket of goods and services. Further, when a nation experiences inflation, domestic price levels increase. A nation's exchange rate must then depreciate to achieve PPP.

The "law of one price" is the basis of PPP. The law of one price specifies that, excluding transaction costs, competitive markets will equalize the price of identical goods in two nations when prices are expressed in the same currency. As an example, the exchange rate for USD/CAD is 1.50. The law of one-price dictates that a camera bought in the United States that cost $200 U.S. dollars should cost $300 if it were bought in Canada. If the camera can be purchased for less than $300 in Canada, it would be more cost effective, excluding transportation costs, to purchase the camera in Canada. If this process of arbitrage were to be carried out on a large scale, such sales would increase the value of the Canadian dollar and make Canadian goods more costly. As a result, sales of American cameras would increase. The law of one price dictates that this process will continue until the two prices reach equilibrium. The law of one price establishes the following:

- Transaction costs, barriers to trade, and other transaction costs can be significant.

- Competitive markets for goods and services must exist in both nations.

- The law only applies to goods and services traded between nations. Immobile or local goods and services such as homes and land are not tradable.

There are two versions of PPP — absolute and relative. Absolute PPP is based on the equalization of price levels across nations as described above. As an example, the exchange rate between Canada and the United States is calculated as follows:

Exchange CAD/USD = the price level in Canada
+ the price level in the United States

The PPP exchange rate requires a price level of 1.5 CAD per single USD. The current exchange rate, however, is 1.13 CAD per single USD. The absolute PPP theory dictates that the CAD will appreciate against the USD and, in return, the USD will depreciate against the CAD until equilibrium is reached.

Relative PPP is based on the rate of change of price levels, otherwise known as the inflation rate. The rate of appreciation of a currency is equal to the difference in inflation rates between two currencies. As an example, Canada has an inflation rate of two percent while the United States has an inflation rate of four percent. The U.S. dollar will depreciate against the Canadian dollar by two percent per year, a theory that holds well when inflation rate differences are large.

One of the simplest methods of measuring PPP between two nations is to compare the price of a standard good, which is identical in both nations. PPP may be measured using a single good as the standard, such as that used in the Big Mac Index, or more sophisticated measurements that look at a group of goods and services. The problem with the latter is that people in different nations tend to consume varying amounts of the same goods and services, making it difficult to compute a truly comprehensive PPP.

BIG MAC INDEX

The Big Mac index is a comparison of the price of a McDonalds' Big Mac sandwich in different countries. It is used to determine if a currency is undervalued or overvalued. If a Big Mac costs $2 in New York and one euro in Spain, the currency exchange rate should be EUR/USD=2. (1 euro=2 dollars) If a trade is executed at EUR/USD 1.5 (1.5

dollars=1 euro), the dollar is considered overvalued and the euro is considered undervalued. The theory of "purchasing power parity" then predicts that the dollar will weaken and the euro will strengthen to make up the difference.

BALANCE OF TRADE

A nation's balance of trade is the most relied on set of figures used in determining the value of a nation's currency. Balance of trade is a measure of the net difference between imports and exports, as measured over time.

The balance of trade in November 2006 for nations around the globe is provided in Appendix F. The U.S. balance of trade with the world is also in Appendix F.

A trade balance deficit exists when the value of imports exceeds the value of exports. Nations that experience regular trade deficits can expect that their currency will fall because a nation's currency is reconverted as it flows in other countries. If more currency is sold than bought, the currency will fall in value. Likewise, a trade balance surplus exists when the value of exports exceeds the value of imports. Nations that experience regular trade surpluses can expect that their currency will rise in value. When a nation experiences a surplus, more currency is sought than is available and the demand pushes up the value of the currency. In reality, however, the balance of trade is not so clear-cut. A trade deficit will only cause a currency to fall if the deficit is greater than expectations. As an example, a country may experience a trade deficit because the country is successful in attracting foreign capital for investment purposes. The currency value rises temporarily, but investors may then hold back because of skepticism over how long the trend will continue. The theory is represented by the J Curve effect.

Point A indicates the current balance of trade or balance of payments (BoP), an initial depreciation of currency and a fall in the currency exchange rate. The depreciation does nothing to improve exports or the trade deficit. In fact, the depreciation increases the amount of currency necessary to purchase imports already obligated for purchase since changes in the currency exchange rate cannot be applied to contracts that have already been signed. In addition, spending on imports rises. As a result, the movement from Point A to Point B indicates that over the short term, an increased trade deficit is experienced to pay for obligated imports. Earnings from exports are not likely to be enough to compensate for the higher spending on imports. However, the movement from Point B to Point C indicates that the balance of trade will improve over the long term as the demand for exports increases and as consumers increase the purchase of domestic goods and services.

GROSS DOMESTIC PRODUCT (GDP)

The gross domestic product is a measure of all economic activity in an economy. The GDP represents the total market value of all goods and services produced by both domestic and foreign companies within a nation's borders. The GDP is a broad measure of economic growth that should range between three percent and five percent for advanced industrialized nations such as the United States, Europe, or Japan. A growth of less than three percent indicates that an economy is stalling and a growth in excess of five percent indicates that an economy is in danger of inflation or a crash. It is not uncommon for developing countries to experience much higher growth rates, but too much growth could cause a fall and create interest rate hikes. Most governments release the percentage of growth in GDP on a quarterly basis.

The GDP of differing nations may be compared by either of the following methods:

- Converting the currency value according to the prevailing exchange rates on international currency markets.

- Converting the PPP of each currency relative to a second selected currency, usually USD.

The relative ranking of nations based on their GDP may differ depending on the approach used for conversion. Nations with less developed economies usually have weak local currencies in comparison to world markets. In less developed economies, the use of official exchange rates may understate the relative effective domestic purchasing power of an average producer or consumer by 50 percent to 60 percent. Though calculations based on official exchange rates may provide misleading indicators for domestic measures, a comparison of GDPs, based on official exchange rates does provide an indication of a nation's purchasing power on the international market.

To understand how economic data affect currencies, traders need to understand the economic characteristics of those markets with the most traded currencies. Traders should be capable of differentiating expected data (or news) from actual data to interpret information properly and analyze the impact on markets. Determining when a market is anticipating news is known as the market discount mechanism. The correlation between a currency market and market news is important in determining currency movements. News that falls in line with expectations will have less of an impact on currency movements than unexpected news. News, whether acquired through the media or government entities, is the primary source of economic data that traders and other market participants use in decision making. News and information provide expectations of the market, which are derived from economic indicators. Specific economic indicators become important in analyzing certain markets. Economic indicators of the major trading markets are of such importance that they should be understood, sought, and analyzed by all market participants.

Important economic indictors for seven markets with the greatest trading volume are outlined below. Those seven markets include the United States, Europe, Japan, Great Britain, Switzerland, Canada, Australia, and New Zealand. The table in Appendix G outlines the important economic indicators for each of these nations.

FORECASTING

Fundamental analysis usually leads to the development of forecasting models, which formulate trading strategies. Such models use various empirical databases in an attempt to forecast market behavior and estimate future prices using various economic indicators established from historical market data. Such forecasts are then used to derive those trades that best exploit the information. These forecasting models are based on a trader's interpretation of the market data, and since each person's interpretation of the same information may differ, there are many and various forecasting models in use. Traders cannot simply adapt an established model. Each trader must study the fundamentals and determine how the analysis fits into the trader's style and expectations.

In forecasting models, the data that comprise various economic indicators are not as important as whether the data fall within expectations for a particular market. Traders need to know not only when and what economic data are published and released but also the forecast for each indicator in the market. For example, the consequence of an increase in the PPI is not as important for short-term trading as knowing what the market was expecting for the month. If the market predicted a drop in the PPI but instead an increase occurred, the increase may lead to inflation over the long term. In the short term, a trader may take advantage of the unexpected rise.

Traders need to know what a market is forecasting for various economic indicators and also the key aspects of each indicator. While unemployment is the headline for the employment index, skilled traders know to concentrate more closely on non-farm employment data since farming data is volatile. Likewise, producer price is the headline figure for PPI; however, skilled traders are more concerned with the value of PPI, less any changes in food and energy prices because food and energy components of PPI are too volatile, so that there is an accurate measure of changes in the PPI.

Revision is a process of modifying economic indicators that have already been published and released. Sometimes when an economic indicator falls outside forecast market expectations, the indicator was incorrectly reported. When this happens, revisions to previously released indicators are published with the next scheduled release. Changes in the current month's reported data may be the result of new market actions as well as revisions to previously reported data. Traders would have to be aware of current and past market conditions to determine which is the case. Traders must be cautious in trading based on economic indicators that fall outside of market expectations because those indicators may need to be revised in the future.

ECONOMIC INDICATORS

Fundamental analysis includes all of the elements that make a nation function, including a mix of government policy, erratic behaviors, and unforeseen events. It is more advantageous for traders, particularly inexperienced traders, to analyze the most influential elements that contribute to the mix rather than attempt to analyze all of the elements of fundamental analysis. Economic indicators are such elements. Economic indicators may affect market prices either directly or indirectly and are compiled and published on regularly scheduled basis to assist market observers to monitor the pulse of the economy. Some of the most important U.S. economic indicators include the gross domestic product (GDP), producer price index (PPI), consumer price index (CPI), industrial production (IP), durable goods, employment cost index, retail sales, and housing starts. These indicators provide a summary of the economic data published by various private and government entities. These compiled statistics have the potential to generate volume and move market prices.

Economic indicators may be divided into two groups — lagging and leading indicators. Lagging indicators are elements of economics that change after an economy has already begun to follow a particular trend or pattern. Leading indicators are economic elements that change before an economy begins to follows a particular trend or pattern. Leading indicators are used to predict changes in an economy.

Analyzing economic indicators requires that traders follow a few simple guidelines to track and organize such data and then make trading decisions based on the information. Traders must be responsible for knowing when such information is released. Schedules of release dates may be found online or acquired from companies that execute trades. As an example, traders may search for economic indicators on the New York Federal Reserve Web site at **www.ny.frb.org**. Keeping track of release dates also assists in understanding unanticipated price and market actions. Price changes may be directly affected following a public release of data or they may be indirectly affected as traders adjust their positions in anticipation of, or in response to, the data.

Traders must understand what particular aspects of the economy various economic indicators are describing. Doing so requires some skill and practice in analyzing the data. The gross domestic product, for example, is an indicator used to measure growth of the U.S. economy, not inflation. If a trader wishes to measure inflation, the trader should be focused on the consumer price, producer price, and employment indices. Some indicators have more potential for moving markets than others. Traders must consider the state of the economy in determining an indicator's potential for moving markets. If the economic growth — not inflation — is a crucial issue for a nation, markets may not react so quickly to changes in inflation data. However, changes in the GDP will be anticipated and could create volatility in the market when such a change is released.

Some investors rely on data compiled and published in the "beige book" of government statistics as an indicator of the direction of the U.S. economy. A beige book of economic statistics from various government agencies is published eight times per year. The book includes data on consumer spending, manufacturing, real estate, new home construction, wages, and employment. The Fed gathers information from the beige book. If statistics indicate a potential problem, such as inflation, the Fed will react to the data. The beige book and other indicators published in the United States are good for U.S. trading strategies, but Forex encompasses a global focus. Other countries also publish economic data, but they may not be as efficient as the G8 in releasing their information. Traders need to find out the specifics of any foreign currency they wish to trade. Not all indicators are created equally, some indicators have more weight in the market and not all are considered to be accurate.

Governments typically spend more money than they take in, and this is not necessarily a bad thing, particularly when the economy is in a recession. The U.S. government distributes money through social programs, contracts, and for emergency situations. Social programs include welfare, social security, unemployment insurance, and disability. Contracts are typically let for security and defense. Emergencies may include natural disasters and terrorist acts. When the government distributes such money, extra money is put into the economy that assists in preventing any downward spiral of the economy that may lead to economic depression. Economic depression occurs when orders for goods and services fall off and companies reduce their workforce. The workers then reduce consumption, causing even more reduced orders and workforce reduction and reduced consumption, a cycle that continues to escalate. On the other hand, the government's distribution of money can be an extremely inefficient method of allocating resources. As an example, governments that let contracts to support projects of constituents that will ensure their reelection or governments that let contracts to relatives and friends may waste money on projects that are ill conceived. As an example, the market may react favorably to a political party that promises tax relief, but if the tax cuts are then perceived as reckless, the market will fluctuate.

Politics are local to a nation, and the government's attitude and stability are essential to the strength of its currency. Some leaders may implement processes favorable to their own country but damage their country's standing in the international market. These leaders are considered anti-market and they may do things such as implement expensive social policy, create barriers to free trade, or default on international loans. Some investors prefer to invest in nations that allow the market to rule rather than the government. The theory is that costs, services, and trade must be brought into balance through markets to acquire some form of stability in currency pricing.

A country's social and political environment also affects the country's currency. The effects can sometimes be simple and other times virtually impossible to recognize. The economic policy of a nation can be subdivided into its monetary policies and its fiscal policies. Monetary policies govern money supply, interest rates, and activities of the central bank. Fiscal policies determine government spending and taxation. Monetary policies define how much control a government may exert over its currency, called managed currency. Fiscal policies attempt to direct the economy.

While governments establish economic policies, a nation's social environment is also critical to Forex and creates the most volatility in market risks. Social change, such as war, revolutions, and peace treaty signings, represent significant events that have a direct effect on markets. Foreign markets have the potential to offer the greatest profit potential and risks. As a result of social change, factors other than economic indicators assist in moving international pricing, making some markets more or less profitable than others. However, the economic health of a country is priced in its currency. Traders must monitor the specifics of each particular country's economics. Economic indicators are only one important method of measuring the health of an economy.

U.S. ECONOMIC INDICATORS

U.S. economic indicators are important in understanding the U.S. dollar; however, the United States is a service-oriented nation, which places specific emphasis on indicators that describe the service sector. Manufacturing accounts for only a small percentage of output. However, the large size of the U.S. manufacturing sector makes the U.S. dollar sensitive to any developments in this sector as well. The Fed differs from other central banks in its mandate to control price stability and sustain economic growth. The Fed uses monetary policy to achieve its goal of limiting unemployment, limiting inflation, and achieving balanced growth.

Monetary policy is controlled with the use of open market operations and federal fund rates. Open market operations include the purchase of government securities such as Treasury notes, bills, and bonds. Such purchases are a signal that policy change will be implemented. In general, an increase in the purchase of government securities signals a decrease in interest rates, while the selling of securities signals an increase in interest rates. The federal fund rate is the interest rate that the Feds charge to member banks. The Fed usually increases this rate to reduce inflation and decreases the rate to promote growth and consumption. The U.S. dollar is the most traded currency in the world, and it has some important characteristics and economic indicators that are recognized in the currency market.

Gross Domestic Product (GDP)

The United States has experienced the highest gross domestic product in the world. About 80 percent of the U.S. GDP is the result of finance, real estate, transportation, health care, and business services. In 2005, the IMF estimate of the U.S. GDP measured more than $12 trillion. U.S. output measured more than three times that of Japan, almost five times that of Germany, and seven times that of the United Kingdom. Foreign investors consistently increase the purchase of U.S. assets because the United States offers the most liquid equity and fixed income markets in the world. The IMF indicates that foreign investments in the United States are about 40 percent of the total global net inflows into the United States. Furthermore, the United States absorbs about 71 percent of net foreign savings. Should foreign investors decide in large numbers to invest or sell U.S. asset holdings in return for higher yielding assets elsewhere, it would create a significant decline in the value of U.S. assets and the U.S. dollar.

The import and export volume of the United States represents about 12 percent of the U.S. GDP. Though this volume accounts for a small percentage of the overall GDP, the United States has the greatest volume of imports and exports in the world, due primarily to the sheer size of the country. Despite the large amount of import and export activity, the United States also maintains a very large deficit that has been problematic for the economy. Foreign funding of this deficit has been weakening since many foreign central banks have considered diversifying their reserve assets from U.S. dollars to euros. As a result, the United States has become more sensitive to changes in money flow. To prevent any further decline in the U.S. dollar, the United States needs to attract a significant amount of inflow.

In 2004, the United States was in need of $1.9 billion per day inflow to offset the existing deficit. The United States is also the largest trading partner for most other countries around the globe. Foreign trades with the United States account for 20 percent of the world's trades. Changes and volatility of the U.S. dollar affect those trades with these other nations. A weakened dollar could boost U.S. exports while a strengthened dollar could curb demand for U.S. exports.

The most important trading partners with the United States include those nations whose growth and political stability have the biggest impact on the U.S. dollar. Leading U.S. export markets include Canada, Mexico, Japan, the United Kingdom, and the European Union. Leading import markets include Canada, China, Mexico, Japan, and the European Union.

The U.S. Bureau of Economic Analysis (BEA) provides two measures of the GDP. One measure is based on income, and the other measure is based on expenditures. An advanced release of GDP is published following each quarter of the year, the most important release of GDP. It includes BEA estimates for data not previously released, trade balances, and inventories. Other releases are considered less significant unless some major revision of the data is included.

Producer Price Index (PPI)

The PPI measures price changes in the manufacturing sector. The PPI measures the average change that domestic producers in manufacturing, agriculture, forestry, electric utilities, natural gas, mining, and fisheries receive in selling prices. The PPIs used most often in U.S. economic analysis are measures for crude, intermediate, and finished goods. Foreign exchange markets tend to focus on the PPI of seasonally adjusted finished goods and the monthly, quarterly, semi-annual, and annual changes.

Consumer Price Index (CPI)

The CPI measures the average price paid by urban consumers for a fixed basket of goods and services. Urban consumers account for 80 percent of the U.S. population. The CPI excludes volatile food and energy components of consumer spending but includes taxes and user fees directly associated with specific goods and services. Price changes are measured in more than 200 categories of goods and services. The CPI is a key gauge of inflation and is responsible for driving lots of market activity.

Industrial Production (IP)

IP is a measure of the change in production for a nation's factories, utilities, and mines. IP is a chain-weighted measure, an index provided by industry type and market type. Referred to as capacity utilization, IP is a measure of industrial capacity and available industrial resources. Manufacturing accounts for one quarter of the economy, and the IP rate indicates how much of the nation's factory capacity is in use. Measured increases in the IP index are usually positive for the U.S. dollar.

Institute for Supply Management (ISM) Index

The ISM compiles a monthly composite index that describes manufacturing activity. The index is based on surveys of 300 nationwide purchasing managers in 20 different industries. Calculated ISM index values above 50 are indicators of an expanding economy, while values below 50 indicate a contracting economy.

Durable Goods and Services

Durable goods and services are a measure of new orders placed with domestic manufacturers for immediate and future delivery. A durable good is a good that lasts more than three years. A durable service is a service that extends for three years.

Consumer Confidence

Consumer confidence is measured by a survey of individual U.S. households. A questionnaire is sent to a representative sample of 5,000 households nationwide, though it is estimated that only about 3,500 households actually respond to the survey. Each of the chosen households is requested to respond to five questions relative to the performance of the economy. The questionnaire asks households to rate business conditions in their local area by providing business conditions within a six-month period, job availability and family income. Responses are then seasonally adjusted with an index applied to each response. A composite index is then determined from the individual indexes. Markets perceive rising consumer confidence as an indicator of higher consumer spending, which is perceived as an indication of possible rising inflation.

Employment Cost Index (ECI)

The U.S. Employment Cost Index (ECI) is an estimated measure of the number of jobs in more than 500 industries in 50 states and 255 metropolitan areas. The estimate considers the number of employees working full-time and part-time in the nation's larger businesses and government. Estimates are acquired through surveys of employer payrolls compiled in the third month of a quarter for the pay period that ends on the twelfth day of the month. The ECI includes wages as well as non-wage costs of employment, which may add as much as 30 percent to the total labor cost.

Employment figures provide an indicator of economic strength since a strong economy creates new jobs. However, if an economy is strong or growing strong and there are not enough people to fill vacancies, companies compete for the best workers and offer higher salaries. Doing so may hurt the economy because fast rising wages create inflation, which may compel the Fed to raise interest rates to cool the economy. As a result, the job market decreases. Likewise, a weak or weakening economy that is unable to create new jobs indicates uncertainty and decreases consumption, which in turn stalls economic growth. However, the weak economy may stimulate the central bank to lower interest rates, creating economic growth. As a result, high unemployment tends to stimulate the market and low unemployment depresses the market. Overall, the U.S. ECI is generally stable, causing very little market reaction.

Non-Farm Employment

Monthly U.S. employment figures are compiled from data taken from two surveys — the Household Survey and the Establishment Survey. The Household Survey provides data for household employment, the labor force, and unemployment rate. The Establishment Survey provides data from non-farm payrolls, the average hourly workweek, and an aggregate hour index. Currency traders tend to focus on seasonally adjusted employment and any change in non-farm payrolls. The non-farm sector of employment is the most important and widely watched indicator. Its relevance to the market is due primarily to political influences rather than economics since the Fed is always under pressure to keep unemployment under control. Interest rate policy is directly influenced by employment conditions.

Retail Sales Index (RSI)

The Retail Sales Index (RSI) is an estimate of the total monthly sales from retailers. The estimate includes samplings taken from retail stores of all kinds and sizes, located throughout the nation. Retail sales include the sale of durable and non-durable goods and services. It includes any excise tax incidental to such sales and excludes any assessed sales tax. It is a measure of consumer activity and consumer confidence. Retail sales provide a timely indicator of broad consumer spending patterns. However, retail sales can be volatile. As a result, they are adjusted for holidays, trading day differences, and seasonal variations. One of the most important sales figures is past auto sales since auto sales may vary from month to month.

Housing Starts

Housing starts are an estimate of the number of residential properties for which construction has begun. A housing start is the beginning of excavation for the foundation of a property. Housing starts include primarily residential properties. Housing is one of the market sectors most sensitive to interest rates and one of the first sectors to react to interest rate changes. Any significant housing market reaction to interest rates indicates whether interest rates are nearing a peak or trough. Housing starts are determined and reported monthly, usually near the middle of month succeeding the published estimate. An analysis of housing starts measures the change in levels from month to month.

Balance of International Trade

The balance of trade measures the difference between imports and exports of trade in goods and services. Trade data is provided for total U.S. trade with all countries along with details for trades with specific countries and regions of the world as well as trades for individual commodities. Trade data examined on a monthly basis has proven to be unreliable so that most traders tend to focus on seasonally adjusted trades, measured over a three-month period.

Treasury International Capital Flow Data

TLC flow data are a measure of the monthly capital inflow into the United States, an indicator used in assessing funding of the U.S. deficit. The TLC and other official measures of inflow and outflow provide an indication of the demand by foreign central banks for U.S. government debt.

EUROPEAN ECONOMIC INDICATORS

The European Union includes 15 member nations. The currency used in all but three of these nations is the euro. The 12 nations that share the euro are collectively known as the European Monetary Union (EMU). The European Central Bank (ECB) dictates the monetary policy of the EMU. The EMU is the second largest economic power in the world, second only to the United States. The GDP was valued at more than $12 trillion U.S. dollars as of 2005. The EMU has highly developed fixed income, equity, and futures markets with the second most attractive market for both domestic and international investments. The Union has a past history of failing to attract foreign direct investment or large capital flows, and it has been responsible for about 45 percent of the total world capital outflow and only about 19 percent of capital inflows because of the ability of the United States to maintain solid returns on its assets. However, the euro has become a more established currency with more nations willing to hold euros in reserve. Capital inflows have increased and demand for the euro has increased.

The EMU is both a trade- and capital-flow driven economy that is also service oriented with no trade deficit or surplus. Exports by the EMU account for 19 percent of world trade exports while imports account for 17 percent of total world imports. The size of EMU trades with other nations provides it with significant power in international trade, its reason for being. The EMU provides for its individual member nations to unite and negotiate under one monetary system, particularly against the United States, which is their largest trading partner. Leading export markets include the United States, Switzerland, Japan, Poland, and China. Leading export markets include the United States, Japan, China, Switzerland, and Russia.

Service oriented sectors of the economy accounted for 70 percent of the GDP in 2001, while mining, utilities, and manufacturing accounted for only 22 percent of the GDP. This is because many companies that produce finished goods outsource their manufacturing activities to Asia while concentrating domestically on research, innovation, design, and marketing.

The EU's growth in international trade has been responsible for bringing about growth in the euro as a reserve currency. It is important for foreign nations to have large amounts of reserve currencies with their major trading partners to reduce the risk in currency exchanges and reduce transaction costs. Before the establishment of the EU and the euro, other nations found it unreasonable to hold large reserves of the individual currencies that existed. As a result, currency reserves were held in U.S. dollars, and most international trades involved the U.S. dollar, British pound, and the Japanese yen. Since the establishment of the EU, many foreign reserve assets have begun to shift in favor of the euro, and this shift is expected to continue as the EU continues expand as one of the major trading partners for nations around the globe.

The ECB has four main categories of open market operations used to influence interest rates, manage liquidity, and signal monetary stance. They include main refinancing operations, longer-term refinancing options, fine tuned operations, and structural operations. The ECB's main refinancing operations provide regular liquidity through reverse transactions conducted on a weekly basis with a maturity of two weeks. This type of open market operation provides refinancing to the financial sector. Longer-term financing operations provide liquidity through reverse transactions conducted on a monthly basis with a maturity of three months. This type of operation provides counterparties with additional longer-term financing. Fine tuning operations are executed on an *ad hoc* basis. The purpose is to manage liquidity in the market and influence interest rates, particularly in an effort to smooth the effects that unexpected liquidity fluctuations have on interest rates. Structural operations involve the issuance of reverse transactions, debt certificates, and outright transactions when the ECB feels the need to adjust the structural position of the euro system via the financial sector. Structural operations may be sought on a regular or irregular basis.

The ECB provides a minimum bid rate, which is the level of borrowing that the ECB offers to member nations' central banks. The rate is subject to change as a result of policy decision making at bi-weekly ECB meetings. Inflation is of great concern to the ECB, and the ECB will intervene in foreign exchange markets if it believes inflation is imminent. As a result, the ECB may keep interest rates at high levels to prevent inflation. The ECB does not target specific exchange rates but recognizes that exchange rates will affect price stability. The ECB factors exchange rates in its policy decisions. Any comments made by the members of the ECB's Governing Council are of concern to market participants since such comments frequently move the euro. The ECB publishes a monthly bulletin that details changes in its perception of economic conditions and its analysis of economic developments. Traders monitor this bulletin for indications of changes in the bias of monetary policy.

Economic indicators for the euro must be combined with indicators of the non-euro member nations of the EU. Traders must analyze the economic and political developments in GDP, inflation, and unemployment for all member countries. Since France, Germany, and Italy are the largest nations in the EMU, their economic data must be analyzed alongside the economic data of the overall EMU.

Gross Domestic Product (GDP)

A preliminary GDP is issued after data is collected from a sufficient number of European countries to produce a satisfactory estimate. Data is usually collected from France, Germany, and the Netherlands. Italy is not included in preliminary GDP data but is added in a final computation of the GDP. The yearly GDP for the 15 nations of the EU and the 12 nations of the EMU is computed simply as the sum of the individual GDPs. However, quarterly estimates require more complex calculations to account for the three nations, Greece, Ireland, and Luxemburg, which do not produce quarterly account data. Further, Portugal produces only partial quarterly account data, which lags in time. As a result, the quarterly computation of GDP for the EU nations and EMU nations is based on data collected from a group of nations that accounts for more than 95 percent of the total GDP of the EU.

Harmonized Index of Consumer Prices (HICP)

An EU HICP is published on a monthly basis. Laws provide that the HICP be designed for international comparisons. A specific index, the Monetary Union Index of Consumer Prices (MUIP), is published for the 11 initial EMU member nations that use the euro. Price data is compiled from each government's statistical agency. Each nation is required to provide 100 indexes to be used in the computation of HICP. The national HICPs are totaled as weighted averages with weights specific to each nation. The HICP is released at the end of the month following a reference period, which is chosen to be about ten days following the publication of national consumer price indexes from France and Spain, the final countries of the EMU to release their CPIs. The HICP release serves as the reference inflation index for the ECB, which strives to keep consumer price inflation in the range of zero percent to two percent.

A broader measure of European money supply is established by the M3. The M3 includes all money supplies to include notes, coins, and bank deposits. The ECB considers the M3 to be a key measure of inflation. The first reference value ever established for M3 was set at 4.5 percent growth in 1998. This reference value provides for inflation below two percent, trend growth in the range of 2 percent to 2.5 percent and long-term decline in the range of 0.5 percent to 1 percent. Growth rate is measured as a three-month moving average to prevent monthly volatility from distorting data from the aggregates. The ECB does not impose limits on M3 growth; therefore, there is no automatic procedure put into place when M3 growth diverges from the reference value. The ECB considers the M3 to be a key indicator of growth, but they also account for changes in other monetary aggregates.

Industrial Production (IP)

IP data includes four major subcategories of production that are seasonally adjusted. These categories include manufacturing, mining, construction, and energy. The manufacturing component includes four main product groups — capital goods, basic and producer goods, consumer durables, and consumer non-durables. The market tends to focus on annual rates of change and monthly-adjusted IP estimates.

Since Germany is the largest country in the euro nations, it is the most important IP figure for traders, though the market also reacts to French IP figures. Initial IP figures are released, subject to revision, based on a subset of the data to be used in the final release. The final release is published when the full data set becomes available. The initial release may also include indicators from the Finance Ministry of the expected direction of the revised data.

Unemployment

Unemployment data is released in Germany, the largest economy in Europe. Data is released monthly by the Federal Labor Office (FLO) along with changes from the previous month in both seasonally adjusted (SA) and non-seasonally adjusted (NSA) data. Non-seasonally adjusted unemployment data include vacancies, the number of employed, and the number of short-shift working arrangements. Within hours of the FLO release, the Bundesbank release of seasonally adjusted unemployment data occurs. Weeks before the release of this data, rumors spread about expectations for the data. These rumors usually quote imprecise data. Comments from German officials are sometimes misinterpreted by the international press. On the day preceding the official releases of data, a trade union source usually leaks the official non-seasonally adjusted data in millions of dollars. When data is reported on Reuters as provided by "sources for the

NSA level of unemployment," the data is official. Traders need to be sure to interpret news reports carefully so that decisions are not made based on rumors and incorrect data.

M3 Harmonized Index of Consumer Prices

As the largest economy in Europe, Germany is responsible for more than 30 percent of the total European GDP. Any insight into German business and economic conditions is considered an insight into the whole of Europe. The IFO survey, conducted by the IFO institute, provides data compiled from more than 7,000 German businesses. The survey requests these businesses to provide their assessment of the German business climate and their short-term plans. An initial publication of survey results includes the business climate headline figure and two equally weighted sub indexes: current business expectations and business conditions. A typical range of indices is 80 to 120, with the high value indicating greater business confidence. Measured values are most valuable when measured against previously compiled data.

Budget Deficits

Individual European nations are governed by the Stability and Growth Pact, which dictates that deficits must be kept below three percent of the GDP. Individual countries set target rates to reduce deficits further. Market participants closely watch failure of these countries to meet their target rates.

BRITISH ECONOMIC INDICATORS

The United Kingdom is the 6th largest economy in the world with a GDP estimate in 2005 of just under $2 trillion U.S. dollars. The United Kingdom has benefited from a history of strong growth, expanding output, low unemployment, and strong consumer consumption. The nation's strength in the housing market is partly responsible for the strength in consumer consumption. The service-oriented economy includes a manufacturing sector that continues to represent smaller portions of the GDP and accounts for about one-fifth of the nation's output. The capital market systems are the most advanced financial systems in the world with banking and finance accounting for the largest percentage of the GDP. Though the GDP is primarily based on services, the United Kingdom is also one of the world's largest producers and exporters of natural gas to the EU. The energy production industry accounts for ten percent of the GDP, which is one of the highest shares of energy production in any industrialized nation. The increasing demand for energy and increases in energy costs continues to benefit the large number of U.K. oil exporters.

The primary U.K. import is finished goods, and the United Kingdom maintains a consistent trade deficit. The largest overall trading partner is the EU that account for more than 50 percent of all import and export activities. On an individual basis, however, the United Kingdom's largest trading partner is the United States.

The United Kingdom has rejected an adoption of the euro as its currency as the government is satisfied that its sound macroeconomic policies have worked well for the country, and rejects the idea of having to adjust its interest rates to reflect equivalent rates of euro nations. The United Kingdom's existing fiscal and monetary policies have outperformed those of most major economies through recent economic downturns, including that of the EU. The U.K. treasury specifies five economic conditions that must be met before the United Kingdom will consider adopting the euro. First, there must be a sustainable convergence of economic structures and business cycles between the United Kingdom and EMU member nations such that U.K. citizens are able to live comfortably with euro interest rates on a permanent basis. Second, there must be enough flexibility to sustain economic change. Third, joining the EMU must create an environment that encourages firms to invest in the United Kingdom. Fourth, joining the EMU must have a positive impact on the competitiveness of the U.K. financial services industry. Finally, joining the EMU must be good for promoting growth and stability in employment.

The politics of the United Kingdom dictate that government officials are very concerned about voter approval. If voters do not support a conversion to the euro, it is not likely that membership in the EMU will occur. Arguments for a conversion to the euro include:

- A single currency would promote price transparency.

- The euro is the second most important reserve currency after the U.S. dollar.

- There would be efficiency in the allocation of capital in Europe through integration of national financial markets of the EU.

- Sustained low inflation under the guidance of the ECB would reduce long-term interest rates and stimulate sustained economic growth.

- There would be uncertainty in exchange rates for U.K. businesses and lower transaction costs and risks.

- U.K. membership with the EMU would increase the political clout of the EMU.

Arguments against a conversion to the euro include the following:

- Historically, currency unions have collapsed.

- EMU criteria, as outlined by the Stability and Growth Pact, are too strict.

- A conversion would require a permanent transfer of existing domestic monetary authority to the ECB.

- Adjusting to the new currency would require large transaction costs.

- The people are anxious about which country would dominate the ECB.

- The lack of monetary flexibility would require that the United Kingdom have more flexibility in housing and labor markets.

- The political and economic instabilities of one nation could affect the euro and negatively affect exchange rates for countries with otherwise healthy economies.

The goal of the U.K. open market operations is to implement changes in the bank repo rate while assuring continued stability in the banking system and adequate liquidity in the market. The bank repo rate is the rate used in U.K. monetary policy to meet targets for inflation as set by the Treasury. This rate is applied to the BOE's own market operations, such as short-term lending. Changes to the bank repo rate affect commercial bank rates for borrowing and saving. Any attempt to increase the repo rate indicates an attempt to cut inflation and any attempt to decrease rates indicates an attempt to stimulate expansion and growth. The goals of U.K. open market operations are in line with the objectives of the BOE. The three primary objectives of the BOE are to maintain integrity and value in the currency, maintain stability in the financial system, and to seek to ensure the effectiveness of the financial services industry. To ensure liquidity, the BOE conducts daily open market operations to sell or buy short-term fixed income instruments of the government. If doing this is not sufficient to achieve necessary liquidity, the BOE conducts additional overnight operations. The United Kingdom is a service-oriented economy with indicators that describe service and non-service sectors of the economy.

Industrial Production (IP) Index

The IP index measures the change in output from the manufacturing, quarry, and mining industry as well as output from electric, gas, and water suppliers. Output is defined as the physical quantity of items produced. It differs from sales volume, which measures quantity and price. The U.K. IP index includes the production of goods and power for domestic sales and export. IP accounts for about one quarter of the U.K.'s GDP and provides an indication of the current state of the economy.

Employment

The U.K. Office of National Statistics conducts a monthly survey, which divides the working age population into three classifications and provides explanatory and descriptive information on each category. These classifications include "employed," "unemployed," and "not in the labor force." The resulting data provide information on major labor market trends, such as unemployment, hours worked, labor force participation, and shifts in employment. The timely, monthly distribution of the compiled data provides market participants with a good measure of the strength of the U.K. economy.

Retail Price Index (RPI)

The RPI is a measure of the change in price of a basket of consumer goods. While market participants are interested in the RPI, they are more concerned with the measure when it excludes mortgagee interest payments. The RPI, exclusive of mortgage interest payments, is called the RPI-X. The RPI-X is used by the Treasury to set inflation targets for the BOE. The current inflation target is set to 2.5 percent of the annual growth in RPI-X.

Housing Starts

Housing starts are a monthly measure of the number of residential building construction starts in a given month. The housing market is the industry primarily responsible for sustaining the nation's economic performance.

Purchasing Manager's Index (PMI)

The PMI is a weighted average of seasonally adjusted measures of output, inventory, new orders, and employment. Data is compiled from a monthly survey conducted by the Chartered Institute of Purchasing and Supply. Index values below 50 percent indicate a contracting economy while values above 50 indicate an expanding economy.

SWITZERLAND ECONOMIC INDICATORS

Switzerland is the 39th largest economy in the world with a 2005 GDP of more than $230 billion. Though a relatively small economy exists, Switzerland is one of the wealthiest per capita economies in the world. Its technological advances and prosperity provide stability that rivals that of other larger economies. Switzerland enjoys prosperity as the result of technical expertise in banking, manufacturing, and tourism; advances in chemical and pharmaceuticals; and precision in instrumentation, machinery, and watches.

Switzerland is also known for a financial system that has historically protected the identity of its investors. These components of the Swiss infrastructure combined with a lengthy history of political stability have created a safe-haven reputation for the nation and its currency. It has also made Switzerland the world's largest destination for offshore capital. The nation is credited with attracting more than 35 percent of the world's private wealth management business and holds in excess of $2 trillion in offshore assets, complemented by a large and highly advanced insurance and banking system that makes up about 70 percent of the Switzerland GDP.

Consequently, the insurance and banking systems employ more than 50 percent of the population. During times of international risk aversion, capital flows tend to drive the economy, while trade flows drive the economy during times of risk seeking. Trade flows are an important aspect of the economy and about two-thirds of all trades are with Europe. Switzerland's leading export markets include Germany, the United States, France, Italy, the United Kingdom, and Japan. Its leading import markets include Germany, France, Italy, the Netherlands, the United States, and the United Kingdom.

Historically, trade flows of merchandise have caused fluctuations in the economy from deficits to surplus. In recent years, the economy has sustained a surplus. In fact, the surplus reached a high of 12.5 percent of the GDP in 2000. With the exception of Norway, Hong Kong, and Singapore, this figure represents the highest surplus experienced by any industrialized nation. The surplus is directly related to the large amount of foreign direct investment. Despite the low yields offered by Switzerland, the safety of capital and privacy in investments lures many foreign investors to invest in the nation.

The Swiss National Bank (SNB) uses Target Interest Rate Range and open market operations to implement monetary policy. Target Interest Rate Range is the target range for its three-month interest rate, known as the Swiss LIBOR rate. The Swiss LIBOR rate is the most important money market rate for Swiss franc investments and is chosen as the target rate. Any change to the rate is documented with an explanation of the change as it relates to the economy of the country. The range typically has a 100 basis-point spread that is revised at least once per quarter.

Open market operations include what is known as repo transactions. A repo transaction involves a borrower and a lender. The borrower sells securities to the lender with an agreement to repurchase securities of the same quantity and type at a later date. Repo transactions are similar to secured loans offered by banking institutions in the United States, where the borrower pays the lender interest on the cash secured by the account. Repo transactions generally have short periods of maturity, usually in the range of one day to a few weeks. The SNB uses these transactions to manipulate undesirable movement in the three-month LIBOR rate. To prevent increases in the LIBOR rate from rising above the SNB target rate, the SNB may provide commercial banks with additional liquidity with the use of repo transactions. Repo transactions would be carried out with lowered repo rates to create the necessary liquidity. The SNB may increase repo transaction rates to reduce liquidity or create an increase in the three-month LIBOR rate.

The SNB provides market participants with its assessment of the current domestic situation through its publications. The SNB publishes a review of monetary policies and a detailed assessment of the current state of the economy in its Quarterly Bulletin. The SNB also publishes a Monthly Bulletin that provides a short review of economic developments.

Gross Domestic Product (GDP)

The GDP, the measure of total production and consumption of Switzerland's goods and services, includes household, government, and business expenditures as well as the net foreign purchases. A GDP price deflator is used to convert current price output into constant dollar GDP. The data are then used to determine where Switzerland falls in the business cycle. Fast growth indicates inflation while low or no growth indicates a recessionary, or weak economy.

Consumer Price Index (CPI)

The CPI is calculated on a monthly basis and is the key measure of inflation. It considers all retail sales paid in Switzerland for a basket of goods. The Swiss computation falls in line with international practice, which dictates that the commodities covered include the goods and services that are part of the private consumption aggregate according to Swiss national accounts. The basket of goods does not include transfer expenditures, such as social insurance, direct taxation, and health insurance premiums.

Production Index

The production index is a measure of change in the volume of industrial production or physical output from producers. This index is released quarterly.

Retail Sales

Retail sales data is published 40 days following the month referred to in the retail sales report. The data is used as an indicator of consumer spending, which is not seasonally adjusted.

Balance of Payments

Balance of payments is used to describe account transactions collectively with the rest of the international community. The current account balance includes the balance of trade plus service portion. The balance of payment indicates the current account balance, which has always been strong. Any change, either positive or negative, is expected to generate substantial flows in the market.

Konjunkturforschungsstelle der eth, Zurich (KoF) Leading Indicators

The Swiss Institute for Business Cycle research publishes a report of the leading KoF indicators, generally used to assess the future health of the Swiss economy. The report contains six components. They include the change in manufacturers' orders and manufacturers' order backlog, manufacturers expected purchase plans for the next three months, construction order backlogs, judgment of stocks in the wholesale business, and consumer perception of consumers' financial conditions.

JAPANESE ECONOMIC INDICATORS

Japan is the third largest economy in the world with a GDP close to $4 trillion in 2005. Japan is also the second largest single economy, and the world's leading exporter, with a manufacturing oriented economy that accounts for about 20 percent of the GDP. Japan exports more than $500 billion in goods per year. Despite its structural deficiencies, Japan maintains a consistent trade surplus, which is responsible for creating a demand for the yen. Japan also imports large amounts of raw materials for the production of goods. The United States and China are its biggest import and export markets. China, being an inexpensive goods producing nation, surpassed the United States in 2003 to become Japan's largest source of imports. Leading export markets include the United States, China, South Korea, Taiwan, and Hong Kong. Leading import markets include China, the United States, South Korea, Australia, and Taiwan.

Japan's open market operations are focused on controlling the overnight call rate. The BOJ has maintained a zero interest rate policy for years. As a result, the Japanese cannot lower rates to stimulate growth, liquidity, or consumption. The only method of manipulating liquidity is through their open market operations. They buy and sell repos, bills, and government bonds with a zero interest target on the overnight call rate. The BOJ has considered implementing methods to address its non-performing loans such as inflation targeting, repacking bad debts and selling them at a discount, and nationalizing some private banks. However, no policy has been decided on or implemented.

Gross Domestic Product

Japan's GDP, a broad measure of total production and consumption of goods and services, is measured and released quarterly and annually. The measure includes total household, business, and government expenditures as well as the net foreign purchases. A GDP price deflator is used to convert current price output into constant dollar GDP. Preliminary reports of the data have been most significant to market participants.

Industrial Production (IP) Index

The industrial production index measures the strength of the manu-facturing, mining, and utility industries. The index includes the production of goods for domestic sales and export and excludes production in the construction, agriculture, transportation, finance, trades, communication, and service industries. It also excludes government output and imports. Each component of the measure is weighted according to its importance during the base period. Market participants examine IP and inventory accumulation as they correlate with total output to gain insight into the current state of the economy.

Employment

The Management and Coordination Agency of Japan compiles and releases employment figures on a monthly basis. Data is obtained from a survey of the current labor force. The release provides an indication of Japan's overall unemployment and the number of available jobs. The timeliness of this release makes it one of the top indicators of economic activity.

Balance of Payments

Balance of payment data includes information on capital flows, goods, services, and investment income. Data is compiled and released on both a monthly and semiannual basis. The figures provide market participants with an indication of international transactions and provide the BOJ with a gauge of international trade.

Tankan Survey

The Tankan survey is a short-term economic survey of Japanese business enterprises. The survey is published quarterly to document results from more than 9,000 small, medium, large, and principal Japanese enterprises to provide an overall indication of the Japanese business climate.

AUSTRALIAN ECONOMIC INDICATORS

Australia has the fifth largest GDP in the Asian-Pacific region, seventeenth in the world, measuring $630 billion dollars in 2005. The relatively small economy has a per capita GDP comparable to many

Western European nations. Australia has a service-oriented economy with about 79 percent of the GDP attributable to finance, property, and business service industries. Manufacturing dominates export activities with rural and mineral exports accounting for more than 60 percent of all manufacturing exports. The economy is sensitive to commodity price changes, and the country maintains a trade deficit. The largest export markets include Japan, the United States, China, New Zealand, and the United Kingdom The largest import markets include the United States, Japan, and China.

Leading exports are with Japan and the Association of Southeast Asian Nations (ASEAN). The ASEAN includes Brunei, Cambodia, Indonesia, Laos, Malaysia, Myanmar, the Philippines, Singapore, Thailand, and Vietnam. As a result, the Australian economy appears to be sensitive to the state of the nations of the ASEAN. However, history has shown that the Australian economy is not only able to withstand an Asian crisis, but also to grow during such a crisis. Australia's sound foundation and strong domestic consumption provide stability for the nation. Consumption has steadily risen since the 1980s. Consumer consumption, rather than exports, is the more important indicator to watch during global economic slowdown.

The Reserve Bank of Australia (RBA) establishes the cash rate as the target rate for open market operations. The cash rate is the overnight rate charged for loans between financial entities. The cash rate should have some correlation with money market interest rates. Changes in monetary policy have a direct impact on the interest rate structure used in the financial system as well as the movement of currency. Daily open market operations focus on managing money market liquidity provided to commercial banks by keeping the cash rate close to the established target rate. To increase the cash rate, the RBA would decrease the supply of short-dated repurchase agreements at a lower interest rate than the existing cash rate.

Australia has maintained a floating exchange rate since the early 1980s. The RBA engages in foreign exchange market operations when the market threatens excessive volatility or the exchange rate opposes underlying economic fundamentals. The RBA uses a trade-weighted index and its cross rate with the U.S. dollar to determine whether to intervene to attempt to stabilize market conditions rather than meet exchange rate targets.

Gross Domestic Product (GDP)

The GDP measures the total production of goods and services in Australia. It includes total household, business, and government expenditures as well as net foreign purchases. A GDP price deflator is used to convert current price output into constant dollar GDP. Fast growth is perceived by market participants as inflationary, and slow growth is perceived as recessionary, or a weakened economy.

Producer Price Index (PPI)

The PPI is a group of individual indexes that measure the average change in selling prices that producers receive for their output. The Australian PPI is released quarterly. The PPI accounts for changes for just about every goods producing industry, including manufacturing, agriculture, forestry, electric utilities, natural gas, mining, and fisheries. Foreign exchange markets tend to focus on the PPI of seasonally adjusted finished goods and monthly, quarterly, semi-annual, and annual changes.

Consumer Price Index (CPI)

The CPI measures quarterly changes in price of a basket of goods and services. It considers a high proportion of expenditures by metropolitan households and includes food, health, housing, transportation, and education. Monetary policy changes affect this index, which is the indicator of inflation.

Balance of Goods and Services

The balance of goods and services is a measure of international trade in goods and services, assessed on a balance of payment basis. This measure is acquired from an assessment of general merchandise exports and imports as reported by international trade statistics compiled from Australian Customs Service records. The information is released monthly.

Private Consumption

Private consumption is a measure of national accounts, which indicates the current expenditure by households and producers of private nonprofit services to households. Private consumption includes the purchase of both durable and non-durable goods. It excludes expenditures for real estate and capital expenditures by unincorporated business enterprises. This measure indicates private consumption, which is a measure of resilience in the Australian economy.

NEW ZEALAND ECONOMIC INDICATORS

New Zealand has a very small economy with a GDP in 2005 of $100 billion. The population of New Zealand is about half that of the city of New York. The nation is shifting from a historically agricultural economy to a more knowledge-based economy with skilled employment and high value-added production. New Zealand has highly developed manufacturing and servicing sectors, but the agricultural sector is responsible for producing most of the nation's exports. The New Zealand economy is trade oriented with exports of goods and services accounting for about one-third of the GDP. The leading markets for both import and export include Australia, the United States, and Japan. Together, Australia and Japan account for 30 percent of New Zealand's trade activity. The small economy and the reliance on trade make New Zealand sensitive to global trading performance, especially the performance of its major trading partners. New Zealand rarely releases economic indicators, but the following are of importance.

Gross Domestic Product

The GDP measures the total production and consumption of goods and services in New Zealand. It includes total household, business, and government expenditures as well as the net foreign purchases. A GDP price deflator is used to convert current price output into constant dollar GDP. Market participants perceive fast growth as inflationary and slow growth as a weakened economy.

Consumer Price Index

The CPI measures quarterly changes in price of a basket of goods and services. It considers a high proportion of expenditures by metropolitan households and includes food, health, housing, transportation, and education. Monetary policy changes affect this index, which is the indicator of inflation.

Balance of Goods and Services

Balance of payments statements record the value of New Zealand transactions for goods, services, income, and transfers with the rest of the international community. The statements also record changes in New Zealand's financial claims on the international community and liabilities to the international community. New Zealand also publishes an International Position statement, which shows the stocks of the nation's international financial assets and liabilities at specific times.

Private Consumption

Private consumption is a measure of national accounts and indicates the current expenditure by households and producers of private nonprofit services to households. Private consumption includes the purchase of both durable and non-durable goods. It excludes expenditures for real estate and capital expenditures by unincorporated business enterprises.

Producer Price Index

The PPI is a group of individual indexes, which measure the average change in selling prices that producers receive for their output. The New Zealand PPI is released quarterly. It accounts for changes for just about every goods producing industry, including manufacturing, agriculture, forestry, electric utilities, natural gas, mining, and fisheries. Foreign exchange markets tend to focus on the PPI of seasonally adjusted finished goods and monthly, quarterly, semi-annual, and annual changes.

CANADIAN ECONOMIC INDICATORS

Canada represents the eleventh largest economy in the world with a GDP in 2005 of more than $1 trillion. The nation has experienced consistent growth since 1991. Traditionally, the economy was based on the exploitation and export of natural resources. Canada exported 22 billion kWh of electricity in 2004. The nation has grown to become the fifth largest producer of gold and the fourteenth largest producer of oil. Even so, nearly two-thirds of the GDP is derived from the service sector, which employs three quarters of the population. The strength of the service sector is partly due to a trend in subcontracting business services. Manufacturing and resources account for more than 25 percent of the nation's exports and provide the primary source of income for a number of Canadian provinces. Canada exports more than 85 percent of its goods to the United States, which makes Canada sensitive to the health of the U.S. economy. The leading export markets include the United States, Europe, Japan, the United Kingdom, and China. The leading import markets include the United States, China, Mexico, Japan, and the United Kingdom.

The Canadian Large Value Transfer System (LVTS) provides the Bank of Canada (BOC) with the framework to implement monetary policy. The LVTS is an electronic platform that allows commercial banks to borrow and lend overnight money to each other so that they may fund their daily transactions. The interest applied to these overnight transactions by the BOC is called the overnight rate or bank rate. This rate is used to control inflation. Changes in the bank rate affect all other interest rates, inclusive of mortgage interest rates and the prime rate charged by commercial banks. The BOC may manipulate bank rates offered to amounts higher or lower than the current market interest rates when the overnight lending rate trades above or below the target. The BOC releases publications that provide indications of the state of the economy at regular intervals. These publications include the Monetary Policy Report and the Bank of Canada Review. The Monetary Policy Report provides an assessment of the current economic environment and provides implications for inflation. The Bank of Canada Review provides quarterly feature articles, speeches, commentary, and important announcements.

Gross Domestic Product

The GDP is the yearly total value of all goods and services produced within Canada. It is a measure of income generated by production, often referred to as economic output. Canada's GDP includes only final goods and services and excludes those goods and services used to produce an end product. This method of accounting for goods and services prevents any output from being counted more than once.

Producer Price Index (PPI)

The PPI is a group of individual indexes that measure the average change in prices that domestic producers receive for their output. The PPI accounts for changes for just about every goods producing industry, including manufacturing, agriculture, forestry, electric utilities, natural gas, mining, and fisheries. Foreign exchange markets tend to focus on the PPI of seasonally adjusted finished goods and monthly, quarterly, semi-annual, and annual changes.

Consumer Price Index (CPI)

The CPI measures the average rate of increase in consumer prices. Usually when inflation is indicated, it presumes that general price increases have caused a decline in the currency's purchasing power. It is usually presented as the percentage increase in the CPI. In Canada, the federal government and BOC establish inflation policy that attempts to keep inflation within a target range of one percent to three percent.

Unemployment

The unemployment rate is released as the number of persons employed as a percentage of the labor force.

Balance of Trade

The balance of trade indicates the nation's trade in goods and services. The balance of trade measures the difference between the value of goods and services exported and those imported. Trades for products, such as raw materials, agricultural goods, and manufactured goods as well as transportation and travel associated with such trades are included in the figure. If exports exceed imports, a trade surplus or positive trade balance is indicated. If, on the other hand, imports exceed exports, a trade deficit or negative balance of trade is indicated.

Consumer Consumption

Consumer buying is a measure of national accounts, indicating the current expenditure by households and producers of private nonprofit services to households. Consumer buying includes the purchase of both durable and non-durable goods. It excludes expenditures for real estate and capital expenditures by unincorporated business enterprises.

6

TECHNICAL ANALYSIS

————

Technical analysis is the most successful and most used method of making decisions and analyzing the Forex market; it differs from fundamental analysis in that it ignores fundamental factors that affect markets and concentrates on price actions of the market. Fundamental analysis can provide long-term forecasts of exchange rate movements while technical analysis has the ability to generate price specific forecasts and information. Technical analysis is primarily used to trade and analyze short-term price movements successfully, establish stop-loss safeguards, and to set profit targets. Technical analysis includes a study of historical price movements in an effort to develop mathematical models or pattern recognition to predict future prices. The developed models and patterns are used to take position in the currency market. Technical traders believe currencies follow very technical patterns in the Forex market, which are due primarily to efficiency in the market, quick trading times — often less than one minute — and the growing number of participating traders. Some technical strategies assume that the fundamental elements of currency trading are already included in a currency's price.

Technical analysis considers four price fields that are available to traders at any given time. These price fields include open, close, high, and low. Most evaluations include charts of price versus time, which emphasize selected characteristics in price motion. Technical evaluations are expected to predict market direction or generate buy and sell indicators. However, trading decisions should never be made on technical indicators alone. A comparison of charts and several different indicators provides the best technical trading strategy.

One of the advantages of technical analysis is the visualization of data. Since history has a habit of repeating itself, technical analysis rejects the belief that market price fluctuations are unpredictable or random. The analysis suggests that when a trend moves in one particular direction, it has a tendency to continue in that direction for some time: minutes, days, or pips. The chosen time is then used for charting and analyzing market data.

CHARTS AND TRENDS

Technical traders typically use charts to display market data to determine market trends as well as important technical indicators, such as points of support and resistance. The proper identification of ongoing trends and recurring patterns that disrupt the continuity of trend lines can be a valuable asset to traders. Charted data that display these patterns can be divided into two categories – reversal patterns and continuation patterns. Reversal patterns indicate that a market entry point is being reached or that it may be time to liquidate an open position. Continuation patterns indicate that a trend was interrupted and then continued in the direction of the original trend.

TRENDS

Market trend is an overall pattern of the market's broad movement. Trend lines are determined by connecting two points on a linear graph of historical data, which describes a particular market. The two points may be either peaks or troughs in the data. Even when the data appears to be a series of ups and downs, a trend line or multiple trend lines may be determined. While two points are often all that is necessary to establish a trend line, a connection of several peaks or troughs provides a more vivid picture of true market trend. Trends may be established for any chosen period, may be sought for minutes, or may be sought over years. They do not necessarily have to represent an upward or downward pattern. The market data may settle into consolidated patterns that do not firmly point in either direction. Many times the data will settle into some of the more familiar charting patterns that will be discussed later.

A common trading technique involves analyzing the intersection of trend lines with the most recent prices. If a downward trend intersects with the most recent prices, it indicates that a trader should buy. On the other hand, if an upward trend line intersects with the most recent prices, the indication is that the trader should sell.

TREND LINES

Trend lines are one of the most controversial topics in technical analysis. Trends are defined by price actions where an uptrend represents higher lows and a downtrend represents lower highs. An uptrend implies that prices are not going down while a downtrend implies that prices are going down. Trend lines provide the simplest tool for determining the direction of a trend. The theory is that in an uptrend traders should draw a straight line that connects the lowest low to the highest high, and in a downtrend traders should connect the highest low to the lowest high. Prices are then expected to fall within these boundaries. The problem is that many traders are confused as to where to draw such lines. Should they choose to draw the lines at closing price highs and lows or the highs and lows of a particular period? Further, should the lines be adjusted to account for spikes in the data, should spikes in the data be ignored, and should the trend lines be adjusted based on the chosen scale of the chart?

Advocates of trend lines agree that trend lines should be used to capture the natural rhythms of buying and selling data. As a result, a more sophisticated use of trend lines involves designing trend line channels. These channels would connect the lows of price actions on one side and the highs of price action on the other side. The strategy would then be to purchase at or near the support trend line and sell at the line of resistance. The objective is to buy cheap and sell at profit several times over the length of a price action.

Doing so can very profitable so long as price remains within the chosen channel. Should the price break out of the channel, traders need to consider several factors and establish parameters for their measurement. Traders need to decide what constitutes a break of a trend line. Piercing the line could constitute a break, or the trader may decide that the price must extend past the trend line. If the price is required to extend beyond the line, the trader must determine by how much the price has to extend. Also, and most importantly, the trader needs to determine if a single break of the trend line for a single price point is sufficient to be considered a true break. Though there is no absolute answer, some rules can be applied with some degree of assurance.

A trend line break is not expected to predict a change of trend, though there are situations where a break signifies the reversal of price action. However, a break in a trend line is simply used to signify that a trend may be ending. What usually follows a break in trend is consolidation, not a reversal of the trend. This is a point of confusion for traders since price actions may generate many false breakouts while still remaining in the same place.

Usually a simple piercing of a trend line during a single period is not considered a true break. A break is more characteristic of a close above the trend line. For example, in the case of a downtrend line, such a close would indicate that buyers have overwhelmed sellers that were initially beating them out. A trend line break requires a price close beyond the trend line. The analysis examines closing prices because the premise of technical analysis is that the past matters but the more recent past is most important. If the price over the next few periods is able to stay beyond the trend line, the trend may be changing. If prices return to the trend line, but then break off again, a change may have occurred.

BAR CHARTS

Bar charts are the most widely used type of chart in technical analysis. They are easy to construct and understand. With bar charts, market activity is represented in daily, weekly, or monthly intervals as vertical bars. Opening and closing prices are represented by vertical marks to the right and left of the vertical bars. As a result, determining market patterns and trends is easy and straightforward. Bar charts provide a method of displaying individual price data elements within a signal time interval without having to link with neighboring data.

The x-axis indicates the chosen time interval and the y-axis indicates price. Each bar represents a single price field. The high and low of a price field for a chosen time interval is indicated by the upper and lower boundaries of the charted bar, respectively. Horizontal rectangles attached to the left side of the bar represent the opening price for the chosen time period. Horizontal rectangles attached to the right side of a bar represent the closing price for the chosen time period.

The horizontal rectangles provide a visual method of displaying the relationship between opening and closing prices within a certain time. A bull or bear may be easily recognized for each time interval of the charted data. In a bull market, the closing price (rectangle extends left) is more than the opening price (rectangle extends right). Likewise in a bear market, the opening price is more than the closing price.

A variation of the OHLC bar chart provides a method of connecting previous quotes with current quotes. This variation, called the Burton System, generates a continuous line to represent price movement. Four basic formations are between two adjacent vertical bars.

There are four basic formations that may result from the two adjacent vertical bars. These formations include bull, bear, outside, and inside formations. The continuous line in the bell and outside formations represent an upward trend. Likewise, the continuous lines in the bear and inside formations represent a downward trend of the associated vertical bars. The second vertical bar of the bull formation has a higher high and a higher low than the first vertical bar. The continuous line connects the lows and highs of both bars such that the start, end, and turning points of the line correspond to the highs and lows of the vertical bars. The other formations share similar relationships.

Bar charts that demonstrate recurring formations have been analyzed, labeled, and categorized in technical analysis. Many investors have tried to develop patterns to predict market behavior with various amounts of accuracy. They have spent much time and effort trying to discern these patterns from the vast array of market data and to understand markets and the trends that move them. Most investors have failed, and some who have succeeded have found that their patterns work temporarily but become useless when market shifts occur. In the process, some patterns have become better known than others. Common formations include lines of support and resistance, head and shoulders patterns, triangular patterns, wedge patterns, channel patterns, and flags and pennants patterns. Certain patterns have become well known to currency traders.

Support and Resistance

All market data will show points of support and resistance and much market activity tends to occur around these points. Traders use support and resistance in determining the placement of stop-loss and profit limit orders.

Support is a price point, which is below the current market price, where buying reverses a downward trend. Support indicates the price at which most traders expect prices will move higher. Support levels are characterized by a sequence of daily lows that fluctuate only slightly along a horizontal line. Support has many buyers. When a support level is penetrated, price drops below the support level. At that point, a support level may become a resistance level. Traders will attempt to limit their losses and sell when prices approach the former level.

Resistance is a price point, which is above the current market price, where selling reverses an upward trend. Resistance indicates the price at which sellers typically outnumber buyers. When a resistance level is broken, price moves above the resistance level.

Head and Shoulders Pattern

One of the most well known reversal patterns is the head and shoulders pattern.

Peaks of the pattern are used to define the shoulders and head. Components of the head and shoulders pattern are defined as follows:

- **Left shoulder** – The market rises and then falls by an amount equal to the rise.

- **Head** – The market rises much higher than before and then falls by amount equal to the rise.

- **Right shoulder** – The market rises and falls again in a shape similar to that of the left shoulder.

A line defined by the troughs on either side of the head is known as the neckline.

Symmetrical Triangle Pattern

The symmetrical triangle pattern is a continuation pattern where market data may be encapsulated in a right triangle.

When the triangle formed is a descending right angle triangle, the pattern favors an upward trend. When the triangle is an ascending, right angle triangle, the pattern favors a downward trend. A line drawn through the troughs of the data forms the base of the triangle. It indicates that declines are deeper than gains. The data encapsulated in the triangle indicates that the price dropped, and buyers sensed that the commodity would be oversold. Buyers then entered the market and pushed the price upward. Sellers saw the gain and sold for profit, pushing the price back down. When the price fell, buyers reentered the market and pushed the price up again. In response, sellers sold and pushed the price down again in a repeating pattern. The overall volume favors sellers, and the price trend is downward. Eventually, buyers decided that the price was unjustified and sold along with the initial sellers, which caused the price to fall to extreme lows. This scenario represents a bear phase. A bull phase would indicate an upward trend with the breakout being through the point of resistance or the point above market price where selling causes a downward trend.

Wedge Pattern

The wedge pattern is a continuation pattern very similar to the symmetrical triangle pattern. Trend lines drawn through the peaks and troughs intersect to form an angle. The angle will point either upward or downward, representing either a bull or bear trend, respectively.

Channel Pattern

The channel pattern is a continuation pattern that usually represents indecision in the market. Trend lines drawn through peaks and troughs are generally flat during periods of low volume. The pattern, itself, usually does not follow the larger trend.

Flags and Pennants Pattern

The flags and pennants pattern is a continuation pattern that also represents a period of indecision, usually in the period after a big move in currency has occurred. Trend lines drawn through peaks usually parallel those drawn through troughs. A currency generally pauses at the flags and pennants pattern and then resumes the direction it was heading before the pause.

CANDLESTICK CHARTING

Candlestick charting is an alternative price charting style that uses solid or empty bar fills to illustrate the ups and downs of market data.

Candlestick charting was established in Japan in the 1700s as a method of charting rice trading. This charting method effectively demonstrates highs, lows, or open and close over a specified time.

The effects are thought to be more illuminating and dramatic than standard bar charts. A candlestick bar is composed of a body and two shadows. The bar fill of the body is empty in a bull market where the closing price is higher than the opening price. Likewise, the bar fill is solid in a bear market where the closing price is lower than the opening price. The body is bounded by the opening and closing price. Shadows are extended above and below the body. The upper shadow indicates the high price for the day, and the lower shadow indicates the low price for the day.

7

THE MECHANICS OF FOREX

C urrency trading is no simple matter and should be given time, an understanding of the market, and a certain amount of self-restraint. Traders must share the global market with other investors, banks, central banks, portfolio managers, and other international financial institutions. The foreign exchange market is a volatile market that does not guarantee a consistent profit. Trading Forex is speculative and can easily result in loss rather than profit. Further, the use of margins in trade increases the volatility of the market. Trading can also be mentally challenging and addictive to some people. Despite advertisements that claim simplicity in the Forex market, traders need to invest considerable time in their trades. The market does not have well defined periods of trade such that the most beneficial trades can be made at any particular time. Moves in trade may happen at any time during the 24-hour period for which the market is open. As a result, traders cannot enter a trade, go about their business, and expect to make a profit. Further, traders are cautioned to trade only with money that they can realistically afford to lose. Successful traders recognize that money management and psychology play an important role in the trading process.

Successful traders in the market are capable of analyzing both fundamental and technical aspects of the market and then make informed decisions based on perceptions of the sensitivity and expectations of the market. Doing so requires staying abreast of market conditions around the globe, educating oneself about the market, and checking various news outlets to monitor changes in the market. Timing is also an important aspect and even the most successful traders have experienced off timing. Successful traders cannot expect to generate a return on every single trade. There are, however, some practices that traders may use to increase the probability of engaging in profitable trades.

MONEY MANAGEMENT

Traders must be capable of managing the money that they trade and determining when it is best to enter or exit a trade. Most trading strategies establish when a trade should be entered, but not all strategies establish an exit. If a trader's strategy does not provide exit points, the trader must establish a method of determining when to exit. Traders may then establish entry and exit points by determining when to take profits and when to set stop losses.

PROFIT AND LOSS (P/L)

Forex trading provides one of the easiest forms of executing and monitoring profit and loss (P/L) in investments. P/Ls in the spot market are generally measured in decimal units. As an example, the value of USD/GBP is 1.4536 at the open of trading. A trader buys one standardized lot, leveraged 100:1. The long position is calculated as follows:

$$\$100,000 \times 1.4536 = 14,536 \text{ pounds}$$

At the close of trade USD/GBP is 1.4542 and the trader sells a standardized lot. The short position is calculated as follows:

$$\$100,000 \times 1.4542 = 14,542 \text{ pounds}$$

The trader sells the unit for more than it was bought. The position profits as follows:

$$14,542 \text{ pounds} - 14,536 \text{ pounds} = 6 \text{ pounds}$$

This profit equates to U.S. dollars as follows:

$$1.4542 \text{ pounds} = 1 \text{ dollar}$$

$$6 \text{ pounds} = 6 + 1.4542$$

$$\$4.12$$

GAINS TO LOSSES

Traders must also determine how large a percentage of winning trades they expect, and they must have some method of predicting the chance of winning to be able to determine how much money to invest in a trade. The ratio of gains to losses assists in determining how much to invest. If trades are providing a high percentage of wins and a higher percentage of gains than losses, an investor need not invest more money in winning trades. While it may be unrealistic to expect 85 percent wins with a 10:1 ratio between gains and losses, most traders would find 30 percent wins with a 5:1 ratio acceptable. Some traders, however, expect a 1:1 ratio and need about 60 percent wins to be able to stay in the trading game.

RISKS TO REWARD

Many traders have a tendency to focus on the reward aspect of trading without taking into consideration the amount of risk involved. The measure of risk taken as compared to reward received is determined by the risk/reward ratio. Consequently, most risk/reward ratios list the reward first. A ratio of 5:1 indicates that the reward is five times greater than the risk. The risk/reward ratio can be quantified by dividing a take-profit spread by a corresponding stop-limit spread. As an example, a trader seeks a risk/reward ratio of 3:1 and takes a long position in JPY/USD based on a fundamental analysis. The current JPY/USD is 1.500 and an analysis suggests that the price will increase to JPY/USD 1.650 within the next 24 hours. No rollover or interest rate differential is required. To receive the 3:1 risk/reward ratio, the trader must set a take-profit order at 1.650 and a stop-limit order at 1.450.

$$\text{Take-profit spread} = 1.650 - 1.500 = 150 \text{ pips}$$

$$\text{Stop-limit spread} = 1.500 - 1.450 = 50 \text{ pips}$$

The risk/reward ratio is calculated as follows:

$$\text{Take-profit spread} / \text{stop-limit spread}$$

$$= 150 / 50$$

$$= 3:1$$

However, if the stop-limit order is executed first, the trader loses 50 pips. If 1 pip = \$100, the profit and loss would be as follows:

$$\text{Profit} = 150 \text{ pips} \times \$100 = \$15,000$$

$$\text{Loss} = 50 \text{ pips} \times \$100 = \$5,000$$

Traders should never allocate more than ten percent of their total investment funds into a single trade as either margin or risk. Traders should also have enough funds for investment that they are able to engage in 30 to 50 different trades. If some trades result in loss, it may be recovered with other trades. If half or more trades result in loss, a trader should analyze and adjust the approach to the market.

LIMITING LOSSES

Traders limit the amount of loss by establishing take-profit and stop-limit orders closer to the market price used on entry into the market. By raising stop-limit orders and lowering take-profit orders, traders may reduce loss potential. If prices create adverse results, traders may eliminate any further potential loss by manually liquidating the trade. If, on the other hand, the price moves are favorable, traders may increase the limits of both orders accordingly. In some instances it may be advantageous to raise the stop-limit order above the market entry price. Doing so guarantees a profit of at least the originally targeted price and at most the newly established price.

In long positions, traders should avoid the lowering of stop-limit orders. They should instead accept a loss and possibly engage in the trade of a different currency pair. Take-profit orders should only be lowered in long positions if a reversal is anticipated. Otherwise, traders should liquidate. Likewise, in short positions traders should avoid increasing stop-limit orders and only increase take-profit orders in anticipation of a reversal. In either case, large losses are usually due to moving and removing stop-loss orders.

Stop-loss orders are typically placed below and above previous highs or lows. However, it may be advantageous for traders to set such stops according to market volatility. Recent charts for traded currency pairs should be examined and the average of sub-trends of the major and minor trend directions should be determined. These averages should be determined periodically to gauge any shift in volatility. The information should then be used to set stops and price objectives. This method may also be used to establish entry points in the market.

PSYCHOLOGY

Almost all people are emotionally attached to their money because one's money is often perceived as one's worth. Forex trading requires traders to detach themselves emotionally from their Forex trading accounts. Losses are guaranteed in Forex, and traders cannot afford to have that loss become emotional stress or a physical illness. However, traders are also cautioned against overconfidence. A profitable trade, especially for novice traders, may lead traders to engage in more trades than they can reasonably track in a trading session. Moderation, experience, and intuition must be used to know when to take calculated risks to succeed in trading.

ANALYZING SELF

One of the first steps in developing a trading strategy involves analyzing oneself for fit in the market. Some of the questions that should be asked of oneself include the following:

- How well do I understand the investment?

- Am I fully aware of the risks involved?

- Am I prepared to dedicate the time and energy necessary to make sound decisions?

- Does the investment fit within my portfolio and investment objectives?

If these questions cannot be answered honestly, one is likely to lose money in currency trading. The risk of this type of investment is high and should really be reserved for investors who are able to absorb any losses that may multiply as the market jumps and dives. It is not a good investment for those with modest incomes and savings. Deciding to become an investor means avoiding the most common mistakes. Not having a plan and attempting to trade against the market are the most common mistakes that new investors make.

If investors cannot explain why they are trading nor what they plan to do in the case of either a loss or profit, it is very likely that they do not have a plan. Trading by instinct almost always guarantees a loss. Hoping that a trade shows a profit is not considered to be a plan.

Another mistake that investors commonly make is trading against the market, which happens when an investor loses and decides to invest more with the expectation that the market will rebound and losses will be recovered. Though this is possible, it is not probable enough to rely on. To ensure more profit than loss, investors should cut their losses on a position when the position takes a loss. On the other hand, if a position is profitable, investors should maintain that position until it hits their intended target. Traders need to have absolute control of their emotions. They cannot get excited over a win or depressed over a loss.

DEVELOPING A TRADING STRATEGY

Trading strategies emerge over time. Each strategy requires the selection of a currency pair to be traded. A trader must then take a position to buy or sell currency, select the number of units to trade, and initiate a trade. There are two options for initiating a trade. A trader may initiate either a market order or a limit order for the trade. A market order allows a trade to be executed at the current market price. A limit order allows trade execution to be delayed until the market price reaches a predetermined limit established by the trader.

A trader also needs to set stop-loss and take profit limits to safeguard the investment. The establishment of stop-loss and take-profit limits is subjective, based on the trader's sensitivity to risk. Some trading platforms will calculate these values for a trader. The calculations may either establish limits as a percentage of the current trading range or as a linear distance from the market entry price. Linear distances are calculated on both sides of the entry price, maybe 10, 20, or 25 pips from the entry price. Traders in open positions have the option of using the calculated values or adjusting them. Stop-loss and take-profit orders are especially important with online trading. If a power outage or computer crash occurs, the market could hit a trader's limit or a price may revert to or below the market price in the time it takes to reboot a computer or recover from a power failure.

ESTABLISH A PLAN

Traders must be prepared to take on the business of trading and not treat it as they would a hobby. They must prepare for any and all possibilities. They should have a plan that includes contingencies and not just hope for the best. Traders must be prepared to make adjustments to, not change, their trading style. They must be poised to take losses but never ride on a losing trade or add to a losing trade. Though some traders consider themselves to be fundamental traders and others consider themselves to be technical traders, a mix of both types of analysis is necessary for successful trading. Any available and valid market data should be used in an analysis regardless of the particular discipline used in generating or gathering the data. An analysis is subjective, and the amount of weight to be put in either discipline will ultimately be determined from experience. Traders may need to modify their strategies, but they should never completely change them because a single trade went wrong.

ESTABLISH POSITIONS

If a chosen position moves unfavorably, the trader is encouraged to do one of two things: allow the price action to trigger a liquidation of the order, or manually liquidate the position before the stop-loss is triggered if it is perceived that the price direction will not reverse itself. What is not recommended is lowering a stop-loss order in a long position, and expecting the price to reverse for a short period of time before moving in the opposite direction. The odds are against this type of price movement.

If a chosen position moves favorably, the trader has many options, depending on price volatility. A significant move of 15 to 20 pips in a long position should signal the trader to move the stop-loss limit above the market entry price by about 3 to 5 pips and raise the take-profit limit by about 20 pips. If the trade continues to move favorably, the trader should continue to raise the stop-loss and take-profit orders, locking in guaranteed profits while the market runs its course. The take-profit limit should not be responsible for triggering an exit from the trade. Market exit should be the result of a reversal that triggers the favorably adjusted stop-loss limit order. The only exception is when the trader feels it is necessary to exit the trade manually.

Pyramiding

A trader needs to be comfortable with how close the two limit orders are set in relation to the current price. By determining support and resistance lines for the price immediately preceding a current price, the trader gets a feel for the range of trading in the immediate past. The process of adding to a favorable open position is called pyramiding, which involves initiating new orders in the same currency pair and in the same position. Experienced traders handle pyramiding best because they are capable of monitoring margin requirements and the balance of their margin account. A margin account may quickly become overdrawn or liquidated by initiating new orders for trades from unrealized profits should a sharp, unfavorable reversal occur.

ANALYZE THE MARKET

Like most other markets, the Forex market requires two major types of trading strategies. One strategy includes a fundamental analysis based on economic factors. The other strategy involves a technical analysis based on price or mathematical factors. Most traders include some of both analytical disciplines in developing their own trading strategy. One of the rules in trading is that the most highly traded currency pairs, such as the G8, tend to move technically, and the more exotic currency pairs tend to follow more fundamental behaviors. However, a combination of both technical and fundamental trading strategies and a good understanding of the market are necessary for success.

A multitude of factors is used in fundamental analysis that could possibly lead to information overload. Some traders are not able to sort through the vast amount of information to come up with a trade. These traders usually resort to methods of technical analysis instead. One of the problems that traders have with fundamental analysis is that it is difficult to convert the qualitative information into specific price predictions. Pending reports, statistical releases, revisions to economic indictors, and other nuisances of fundamental data will often cause violent market reactions in one direction. Also, the leverage allowed in Forex makes it difficult to accept reports of a bull or bear market without being able to attach specific values to currencies. A technical analysis is thought to transform all the fundamental factors that influence the market into a simple tool, called prices. However, traders who opt for technical analysis cannot completely ignore the fundamentals of trading. Without knowing the particulars of a market and its underlying elements, a trader trades on luck, good or bad.

A good trading strategy requires one or both types of analysis, but those are not the only components of a good trading system. Psychology and money management play a role in trading decisions. Analyses provide a trader with information and indicators to define entry and exit points, but it is the psychology and money management components of trading that cause a trader to fail to act on the resulting analysis. Most traders devote their time to developing a trading strategy, but the most successful traders insist that strategy is the least important component. They insist that more traders would do better to allocate more focus on the other two components — psychology and money management.

DETERMINE VOLATILITY

Novice traders should begin to trade with the major currencies, particularly those currency pairs that include the USD. These currency pairs usually require lower transaction costs and lower bid/ask spreads that increase profit potential.

The foreign exchange market operates 24 hours a day. Traders find it impossible to track all market movements or to respond to movements at all times; however, timing is very important to currency trading. If a trader wants to develop an effective and time efficient strategy, the trader needs to be aware of global market activity to maximize the trading opportunities available during trading hours. A currency pair's trading range is dependent on geographical location and macroeconomic factors. A trader needs to know what time of day a particular currency pair experiences the widest or narrowest trading range so that they may allocate investment capital accordingly. Traders need some insight into the trading activities of currency pairs in different time zones. They also need insight into when those pairings are most volatile.

European Trading Session

The London market offers such high liquidity and efficiency that the majority of foreign exchange transactions are completed during the London market hours of 2 a.m. to 12 p.m. EST. The large number of market participants and high transaction values make the London market the most volatile foreign exchange market in the world. London has the largest and most important dealing center with a market share of about 30 percent. Most of the dealing desks of large banks are located in London.

For example, half of the currency pairs surpass the 80 pips line. Eighty pips is the benchmark used for establishing volatile pairs. The GBP/CHF and GBP/JPY pairs are appealing to the most risk tolerant traders because the daily ranges average more than 140 pips. These pairs can be used to generate huge profits in short amounts of time. The high volatility is due to the peak in daily trade activities since large market participants complete their cycle of currency conversions around the globe during this time.

There is a direct connection between London trading hours and the U.S. and Asian trading hours. As large banks and institutional investors finish repositioning their portfolios, they need to convert their European assets into dollar-dominated assets in anticipation of the U.S. market opening. These conversions by the big market participants are responsible for the extreme volatility in the GBP/CHF and GBP/JPY pairs.

The four pairs, USD/CHF, GBP/USD, USD/CAD and EUR/USD are more appealing to the most risk tolerant traders. These four pairs have an average range of 100 pips. Their high volatility provides traders with a number of opportunities to enter the market. These pairs are more appealing to the most risk aversion market participants because they average about 50 pips and provide traders with high profit potential as well as interest income. Investors may determine the direction of movements based on fundamental economic factors, making them less prone to losses from intraday speculative trades.

U.S. Trading Session

The New York trading session is between 8 a.m. and 5 p.m. EST. The majority of transactions occurs between 8 a.m. and noon. This time offers high liquidity because the European market is still in session. New York has the second largest foreign exchange market in the world.

The GBP/CHF, GBP/JPY USD/CHF and GBP/USD pairs offer the broadest range, reaching more than 80 pips. These four pairs are appealing to the most risk tolerant day traders since the daily ranges average about 120 pips. Increased activity in these pairs is due to the fact that transactions directly involve the U.S. dollar. Foreign investors must convert their domestic currency to dollar-dominated assets to engage in transactions in the U.S. equity and bond markets.

Most currencies in the foreign exchange market are quoted in U.S. dollars, usually the base currency. These currencies are then traded against the U.S. dollar before being translated into other currencies. In the case of GBP/CHF, the British pound is traded against the U.S. dollar and then converted to Swiss francs. The trade involves two transactions, GBP/USD and USD/CHF. The volatility is determined by the correlation of the two derived currency pairs. This correlation determines how closely the two currencies move in the same direction. A negative correlation signifies that the currencies are moving in opposite directions. (If GBP/USD and USD/CHF have negative correlations, the volatility of GBP/CHF is increased.) Trading currency pairs that have high volatility offers high profit potential, but it also offers high risk. Traders need to revise their strategy continually in response to market conditions because abrupt movements in exchange rates have the potential to stop their trading orders or nullify long-term strategies.

The USD/CAD, EUR/USD and USD/JPY pairs are more appealing to risk aversion traders since these pairs offer a fair amount of range to make profit with a smaller amount of risk. The high liquidity allows investors to gain profits or cut their losses immediately and efficiently. The modest volatility provides an environment for traders to pursue long-term strategies.

Asian Trading Session

Foreign exchange trades during the Asian trading session occur between 7 p.m. and 4 a.m. EST. Trades are conducted in regional financial hubs, with Tokyo having the largest market share. Hong Kong and Singapore have the second and third largest share, respectively.

The BOJ has strong influences on the foreign exchange market, but Tokyo is one of the most important dealing centers. Some market participants use the trade momentum of the Tokyo market to gauge market dynamics and devise trading strategies. Hedge funds and large investment banks may use the Asian session to implement stops and option barrier levels.

The GBP/JPY, GBP/CHF, and USD/JPY pairs offer the broadest range, reaching close to or exceeding 80 pips. These three pairs are appealing to the most risk tolerant and short-term traders because the broad range provides profit potential that averages about 90 pips. The three pairs, USD/CHF, GBP/USD, and AUD/JPY are more appealing for medium to long-term traders because these trades allow traders to factor fundamentals into their decision-making. The less moderate volatility of these pairs assists in shielding traders and their strategies from the potential of irregular market movement resulting from intraday speculative trades.

Institutional investors and foreign investment banks generate a significant volume of USD/JPY transactions as they position themselves to enter the Japanese bond and equity markets. The majority of assets held by these financial entities is dollar-dominated and must be converted into Japanese yen before entering the Japanese markets. Through its open market operations, the Bank of Japan has an influential role in the supply and demand of USD/JPY. The central bank holds more than $800 billion in U.S. Treasury securities. Large Japanese exporters who also need to convert their foreign earnings play a role in the increasing the volume of USD/JPY transactions during the Tokyo trading hours.

GBP/CHF and GBP/JPY are highly volatile since big market participants and central bankers take positions in anticipation of the opening of the European session.

TRADING SESSION OVERLAPS

The foreign exchange market tends to be more active when markets overlap, particularly when the two largest trading centers, U.S. and European, overlap.

United States – European Trading Sessions Overlap

The range of trading between 8 a.m. and noon EST accounts, on average, for 70 percent of the average trading for all currency pairs during the European session and 80 percent of the average trading for all currency pairs during the U.S. session. Day traders who seek wide ranges and volatile price actions find this to be a good time to trade.

European – Asian Trading Session Overlap

The range of trading between 2 a.m. and 4 a.m. is lower than any other trading session because of the slow trading in the early Asian trading hours. Risk tolerant traders may ignore these thin trading hours or use the time to position themselves for a breakout move when the U.S. or European markets open.

DETERMINE TRENDS

As part of the strategy for trading, traders must be capable of evaluating the market and determining whether trends are moving upward or downward, are weakening or strengthening, are newly formed or long standing, or are in a good trading range. Successful traders do not gauge trade pricing as too high or too low, they gauge the price of one currency relative to another. They need a clear picture of market situations. No matter how complex or simple a trader's trading system may be, a trader benefits from charted market data. Charts provide insight into trends and time series ranges. Traders must be capable of analyzing and interpreting charted data since different trends may be observed from charts of the same data with differing scales. Traders must then determine what they would do if prices open higher or lower than expected, if the market is quiet or volatile, if the market experiences new highs or new lows, or if the market experiences highs or lows early and then reverses.

Trends in the market are best realized by studying charts of market data. Some important indicators in charted data include the length of primary versus secondary trends, average times between trend tops and bottoms, and the average range charted over various time intervals. Charting data for the same market on different scales also provides a good perspective on market trends. Data charted over minutes or hours may provide a much different perspective than data charted daily. Price movement and volatility may also be charted. Also referred to as a trend slope, price movement is the slope of a trend measured from the beginning point to the end point. Volatility is the total amount of price movement over a specified time.

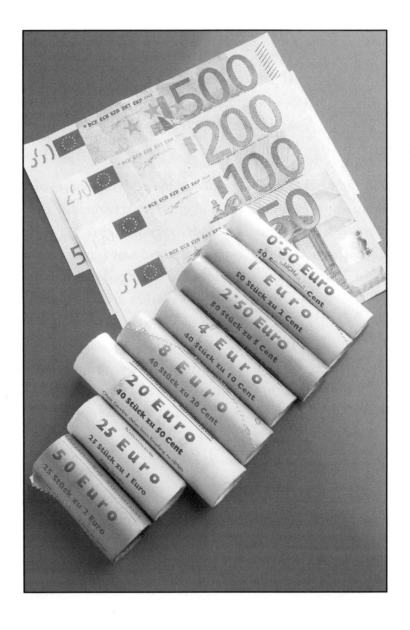

CONCLUSION

———

While currency trading and the Forex market are sometimes advertised as simple "get rich" techniques, success in currency trading requires a demanding level of skill, patience, and time that may only be appealing to certain personalities. As with many other aspects of society, the number-crunching capabilities of computers have extended access to trading markets to a larger group of individuals.

Computers have provided methods of trading in a market that was historically limited to large banks and financial institutions. However, traders in the currency market need to have certain analytical skills or the propensity to develop such analytical skills to be able to apply some of the complex methods involved in currency trading. Relatively speaking, electronic methods of currency trading are still in their technological infancy. As a result, controls and safeguards, including those usually implemented by governmental bodies, have not been implemented to protect investors from unforeseen loss or manipulation by other more experienced market participants. The nature of the market as opposed to electronic mechanisms has prevented large banks and financial institutions from completely controlling and dominating the market. However, these institutions are still poised to manipulate the market and market pricing. This edge has effectively tricked and weeded out inexperienced, unsuspecting market participants.

Success in the Forex trading market depends on one's ability to interpret information and then perform an analysis of that information. Trading and investing requires a certain amount of discipline, expert analysis, and risk. Unlike the banking world, where deposits are guaranteed by the federal government, stocks, bond currencies, and other securities can lose value. Traders trade at their own risk. Methods, tactics, and strategies have been developed to assist traders in minimizing the risks; however, these methods, tactics, and strategies must be practiced, studied, and tried until a successful strategy is developed in the best interest of the trader.

Interest rates and interest rate differentials are an important aspect of currency trading, but traders must also be capable of choosing the most profitable currency pairs to trade. Doing so requires a thorough understanding of economic impacts, monetary policies, and market timing. The foreign exchange market offers volatility that cannot always be predicted, but knowledgeable traders will be capable of reacting to it properly. The fundamental analysis of currency trading considers those social, political, and economic factors that influence the market. These factors are used as forecasting tools to predict market movement. The technical analysis of currency trading examines historical price movements in an effort to predict future price movements. Price movements are expected to follow trends and patterns recognizable in historical data. As a smart trader, you will combine both analytical methods in determining appropriate entry and exit in the foreign exchange market.

CASE STUDY: MARK L. WAGGONER

Can you relate particularly interesting, successful experiences you have had in currency trading?

In 2000–2004 rates in the United States were dropping. Major currencies rallied as the U.S. dollar drifted lower. This is the classic example of following interest rates. Literally thousands could have been made over the course of two or three years.

Can you list the steps one must take to enter currency trading?

First and foremost, do your homework! I like to look at what countries are raising rates (buy) and which are lowering rates (sell). Look for established trends. There's not really a whole lot to it if you're playing long-term trends. If you are playing short term it becomes MUCH more complicated. Time to do more homework!

Does a currency trader need to be in a large city or can anyone with an Internet connection enter the field?

Anyone with an Internet connection will be able to trade. I do not even suggest trading without it because you need the frequently updated news and information. It's much faster than television or newspapers.

Which currencies traditionally do well when traded?

Any major currencies can be traded. To start, stay with the most common.

What would you advise someone who is just starting out as a currency trader?

Watch trends and buy if a market is going up; sell if the market is going down.

How much of an investment would you recommend that a person have on hand before launching a currency trading business?

We recommend a minimum of $10,000. Statistically your chances of making money are dramatically increased. Remember ALWAYS leave

CASE STUDY: MARK L. WAGGONER

50 percent of your funds on the sideline for adverse price movement and ALWAYS use stops!

Wait for trades to come to you. Most trades will present themselves. Just because you opened an account does not mean you have to trade that day. Check, recheck, and then enter a market. Have a plan that is written for each trade that includes:

• Entry Point

• Stop

• Exit Strategy

When the trade is right, you'll know and enter the market.

Mark L. Waggoner

President

Excel Futures, Inc.

16691 Gothard Street, Suite #L

Huntington Beach, CA. 92647

http://www.excelfutures.com

Toll Free: (888) 959-9955 / International: 01-714-843-9884

REFERENCES

1. Archer, Michael. Getting Started in Currency Trading: Winning in Today's Hottest Marketplace.

2. Brown, Kedrick. Trend Trading: Timing Market Tides. Wiley Trading

3. Lien, Kathy. Forex Revolution: Day Trading the Currency Market: Technical and Fundamental Strategies To Profit from Market Swings. Willey Trading

4. Rosenstreich, Peter. Forex Revolution: An Insider's Guide to the Real World of Foreign Exchange Trading. Financial Times Prentice Hall Books.

5. Schlossberg, Boris. Technical Analysis of the Currency Market: Classic Techniques for Profiting from Market Swings and Trader Sentiment. Wiley Trading

APPENDIX

APPENDIX A: INTERNATIONAL CURRENCIES

The table includes the currency, its Forex symbol, country, and country code.

Country	Currency Code	Currency	Country Code
	XCD	East Caribbean Dollar	AI
Afghanistan	AFA	Afghani	AF
Albania	ALL	Lek	AL
Algeria	DZD	Algerian Dinar	DZ
American Samoa	USD	US Dollar	AS
Andorra	EUR	Euro	AD
Angola	AON (replacement for AOK)	New Kwanza (replacement for Kwanza)	AO
Antigua and Barbuda	XCD	East Caribbean Dollar	AG
Argentina	ARA, ARS (replacement for ARP)	Austral and Argenintinian Nuevo Peso (replacement for the Peso)	AR
Armenia	AMD	Dram (Russian Ruble [RUR] was formerly in use)	AM
Aruba	AWG	Aruban Florin	AW
Australia	AUD	Australian Dollar	AU

Country	Currency Code	Currency	Country Code
Austria	EUR	Euro	AT
Azerbaijan	AZM	Azerbaijani Manat (Russian Ruble [RUR] was formerly in use)	AZ
Bahamas	BSD	Bahamian Dollar	BS
Bahrain	BHD	Bahraini Dinar	BH
Bangladesh	BDT	Taka	BD
Barbados	BBD	Barbados Dollar	BB
Belarus (formerly known as Byelorussia)	BYR	Belarussian Ruble (Russian Ruble [RUR] was formerly in use)	BY
Belgium	EUR	Euro	BE
Belize	BZD	Belize Dollar	BZ
Benin	XAF	Communauté Financière Africaine Franc	BJ
Bermuda	BMD	Bermudian Dollar	BM
Bhutan	BTN (also INR)	Ngultrum (Indian Rupee also circulates)	BT
Bolivia	BOB, BOP	Bolivian Boliviano	BO
Bosnia & Herzegovina	BAM	Convertible Mark	BA
Botswana	BWP	Pula	BW
Brazil	BRL	Cruzeiro Real	BR
British Indian Ocean Territory	GBP, SCR	Pound Sterling (United Kingdom Pound), Seychelles Rupee	IO
Brunei Darussalam	BND	Brunei Dollar	BN
Bulgaria	BGL	Bulgarian Lev	BG

Country	Currency Code	Currency	Country Code
Burkina Faso	XAF	Communauté Financière Africaine Franc	BF
Burundi	BIF	Burundi Franc	BI
Cambodia (formerly Kampuchea)	KHR	Riel	KH
Cameroon	XAF	CFACentral African Franc	CM
Canada	CAD	Canadian Dollar	CA
Cape Verde	CVE	Escudo Caboverdiano	CV
Cayman Islands	KYD	Cayman Islands Dollar	KY
Central African Republic	XAF	Communauté Financière Africaine Franc	CF
Chad	XAF	Communauté Financière Africaine Franc	TD
Chili	CLP	Chilean Peso	CL
China	CNY	Yuan Renminbi	CN
Christmas Island	AUD	Australian Dollar	CX
Cocos (Keeling) Islands	AUD	Australian Dollar	CC
Colombia	COP	Colombian Peso	CO
Comoros	KMF	Comorian Franc	KM
Congo, Democratic Republic of the (formerly Zaïre)	CDZ (formerly ZRZ)	New Zaïre	CD (formerly ZR)
Congo-Brazzaville	XAF	Franc	CG

Country	Currency Code	Currency	Country Code
Congo-Kinshasa	CDF	Congolese Franc	CG
Cook Islands	NZD	New Zealand Dollar	CK
Costa Rica	CRC	Costa Rican Colón	CR
Cuba	CUP	Cuban Peso	CU
Cyprus	CVP	Cypriot Pound	CY
Czech Republic	CZK	Czech Koruna	CZ
Denmark	DKK	Danish Krone	DK
Djibouti	DJF	Djibouti Franc	DJ
Dominica	XCD	East Caribbean Dollar	DM
Dominican Republic	DOP	Dominican Republic Peso	DO
East Timor	TPE	Timorian Escudo, American and Australian Dollar	TP
Ecuador	USD (ECS)	US Dollar (superseded Sucre in 2000)	EC
Egypt	EGP	Egyptian Pound	EG
El Salvador	SVC	El Salvadorian Colón	SV
Equatorial Guinea	XAF, GQE	Franc de la Communauté Financière Africaine and Ekwele	GQ
Eritrea	ERN, ETB	Eritrean Nakfa, Ethiopian Birr	ER
Estonia	EEK	Kroon	EE
Ethiopia	ETB	Birr	ET
European Community	EUR (formerly XEU)	Euro (formerly known as the ECU)	??

Country	Currency Code	Currency	Country Code
Falkland Islands (Malvinas)	FKP	Falkland Pound	FK
Faroe Islands	DKK	Danish Krone	FO
Fiji Islands	FJD	Fiji Dollar	FJ
Finland	EUR	Euro	FI
France	EUR	Euro	FR
France, Metropolitan	EUR	Euro	FX
French Guiana	EUR	Euro	GF
French Polynesia	XPF	Franc des Comptoirs Français du Pacifique	PF
French Southern and Antarctic Territories	EUR	Euro	TF
Gabon	XAF	Communauté Financière Africaine Franc	GA
Gambia	GMD	Dalasi	GM
Georgia	GEL	Lari (Russian Ruble [RUR] was formerly in use)	GE
Germany (West and East)	EUR	Euro	DE (formerly DE for West and DD for East)
Ghana	GHC	Cedi	GH
Gibraltar	GIP	Gibraltar Pound	GI
Greece	EUR	Euro	GR
Greenland	DKK	Danish Krone	GL
Grenada	XCD	East Caribbean Dollar	GD

Country	Currency Code	Currency	Country Code
Guadeloupe	EUR	Euro	GP
Guam	USD	US Dollar	GU
Guatemala	GTQ	Quetzal	GT
Guinea	GNS	Guinea Syli (also known as Guinea Franc)	GN
Guinea-Bissau	GWP, XAF	Guinea-Bissau Peso and Franc de la Communauté Financière Africaine	GW
Guyana	GYD	Guyana Dollar	GY
Haiti	HTG	Gourde	HT
Heard and McDonald Islands	AUD	Australian Dollar	HM
Holy See (Vatican City State)	EUR	Euro	VA
Honduras	HNL	Lempira	HN
Hong Kong	HKD	Hong Kong Dollar	HK
Hungary	HUF	Forint	HU
Iceland	ISK	Icelandic Króna	IS
India	INR	Indian Rupee	IN
Indonesia	IDR	Rupiah	ID
Iran, Islamic Republic of	IRR	Iranian Rial	IR
Iraq	IQD	Iraqi Dinar	IQ
Ireland	EUR	Euro	IE
Israel	ILS	Israeli New Shekel	IL
Italy	EUR	Euro	IT
Ivory Coast (Côte d'Ivoire)	XAF	Communauté Financière Africaine Franc	CI
Jamaica	JMD	Jamaican Dollar	JM
Japan	JPY	Yen	JP

Country	Currency Code	Currency	Country Code
Jordan	JOD	Jordanian Dinar	JO
Kazakhstan	KZT	Tenge (Russian Ruble [RUR] was formerly in use)	KZ
Kenya	KES	Kenyan Shilling	KE
Kiribati	AUD	Australian Dollar	KI
Korea, Democratic People's Republic of (North Korea)	KPW	North Korean Won	KP
Korea, Republic of (South Korea)	KRW	South Korean Won	KR
Kuwait	KWD	Kuwaiti Dinar	KW
Kyrgyzstan	KGS	Kyrgyzstani Som	KG
Lao People's Democratic Republic (formerly Laos)	LAK	Kip	LA
Latvia	LVL	Lats	LV
Lebanon	LBP	Lebanese Pound	LB
Lesotho	LSL, LSM, ZAR	Loti, Maloti and South African Rand	LS
Liberia	LRD	Liberian Dollar	LR
Libyan Arab Jamahiriya	LYD	Libyan Dinar	LY
Liechtenstein	CHF	Swiss Franc	LI
Lithuania	LTL	Litas	LT
Luxembourg	EUR	Euro	LU

Country	Currency Code	Currency	Country Code
Macao (also spelled Macau)	MOP	Pataca	MO
Macedonia, the Former Yugoslav Republic of	MKD	Macedonian Denar	MK
Madagascar	MGF	Madagascar (Malagasi) Franc	MG
Malawi	MWK	Malawian Kwacha	MW
Malaysia	MYR	Ringgit (Malaysian Dollar)	MY
Maldives	MVR	Rufiyaa	MV
Mali	XOF	Franc de la Communauté Financière Africaine and Malian Franc	ML
Malta	MTL (MTP formerly in use)	Maltese Lira (Maltese Pound formerly in use)	MT
Marshall Islands	USD	US Dollar	MH
Martinique	EUR	Euro	MQ
Mauritania	MRO	Ouguiya	MR
Mauritius	MUR	Mauritius Rupee	MU
Mayotte	EUR	Euro	YT
Mexico	MXN (replacement for MXP)	Mexican New Peso (replacement for Mexican Peso)	MX
Micronesia, Federated States of	USD	US Dollar	FM

Country	Currency Code	Currency	Country Code
Moldova, Republic of	MDL	Moldovian Leu	MD
Monaco	EUR	Euro	MC
Mongolia	MNT	Tugrik	MN
Montserrat	XCD	East Caribbean Dollar	MS
Morocco	MAD	Moroccan Dirham	MA
Mozambique	MZM	Metical	MZ
Myanmar (formerly Burma)	MMK (formerly BUK)	Kyat	MM (formerly BU)
Namibia	NAD, ZAR	Namibian Dollar and South African Rand	NA
Nauru	AUD	Australian Dollar	NR
Nepal	NPR	Nepalese Rupee	NP
Netherlands	EUR	Euro	NL
Netherlands Antilles	ANG	Netherlands Antilles Guilder (Florin)	AN
New Caledonia	XPF	Franc des Comptoirs Français du Pacifique	NC
New Zealand	NZD	New Zealand Dollar	NZ
Nicaragua	NIO	Córdoba Oro	NI
Niger	XOF	West African Franc and Franc de la Communauté Financière Africaine	NE
Nigeria	NGN	Naira	NG
Niue	NZD	New Zealand Dollar	NU
Norfolk Island	AUD	Australian Dollar	NF
Northern Mariana Islands	USD	US Dollar	MP
Norway	NOK	Norwegian Krone	NO

Country	Currency Code	Currency	Country Code
Oman	OMR	Rial Omani	OM
Pakistan	PKR	Pakistani Rupee	PK
Palau	USD	US Dollar	PW
Panama	PAB, USD	Balboa and US Dollar	PA
Papua New Guinea	PGK	Kina	PG
Paraguay	PYG	Guarani	PY
Peru	PEI, PEN (PEN replaced PES)	Nuevo Sol (New Sol replaced Sol)	PE
Philippines	PHP	Philippines Peso	PH
Pitcairn Island	NZD	New Zealand Dollar	PN
Poland	PLN (replacement for PLZ)	New Zloty (replacement for Zloty)	PL
Portugal	EUR	Euro	PT
Puerto Rico	USD	US Dollar	PR
Qatar	QAR	Qatari Riyal	QA
Réunion	EUR	Euro	RE
Romania	ROL	Romanian Leu	RO
Russian Federation	RUB (formerly RUR)	Russian Federation Ruble	RU
Rwanda	RWF	Rwanda Franc	RW
Saint Kitts (Christopher) and Nevis	XCD	East Caribbean Dollar	KN
Saint Lucia	XCD	East Caribbean Dollar	LC
Saint Vincent and the Grenadines	XCD	East Caribbean Dollar	VC

Country	Currency Code	Currency	Country Code
Samoa	WST	Tala	WS
San Marino	EUR	Euro	SM
São Tomé and Príncipe	STD	Dobra	ST
Saudi Arabia	SAR	Saudi Riyal	SA
Senegal	XOF	West African Franc and Franc de la Communauté Financière Africaine	SN
Serbia	RSD	Dinar	CS
Serbia and Montenegro (formerly in Yugoslavia)	CSD, EUR	Serbian Dinar (Serbia), Euro (Montenegro), Euro (Kosovo & Metohia)	CS
Seychelles	SCR	Seychelles Rupee	SC
Sierra Leone	SLL	Leone	SL
Singapore	SGD	Singapore Dollar	SG
Slovakia (Slovak Republic)	SKK	Slovak Koruna	SK
Slovenia	EUR	Euro	SI
Solomon Islands	SBD	Solomon Islands Dollar	SB
Somalia	SOS	Somali Shilling	SO
South Africa	ZAR	Rand	ZA
South Georgia and the South Sandwich Islands	GBP	Pound Sterling	GS
Spain	EUR	Euro	ES
Sri Lanka	LKR	Sri Lankan Rupee	LK
St Helena	SHP	St Helenian Pound	SH

Country	Currency Code	Currency	Country Code
St Pierre and Miquelon	EUR	Euro	PM
Sudan	SDP, SDD	Sudanese Pound and Sudanese Dinar	SD
Suriname	SRG	Surinam Guilder (also known as Florin)	SR
Svalbard and Jan Mayen Islands	NOK	Norwegian Krone	SJ
Swaziland	SZL	Lilangeni	SZ
Sweden	SEK	Swedish Krona	SE
Switzerland	CHF	Swiss Franc	CH
Syrian Arab Republic	SYP	Syrian Pound	SY
Taiwan	TWD	New Taiwan Dollar	TW
Tajikistan	TJR	Tajik Ruble (Russian Ruble [RUR] was formerly in use)	TJ
Tanzania, United Republic of	TZS	Tanzanian Shilling	TZ
Thailand	THB	Baht	TH
Togo	XOF	Communauté Financière Africaine Franc	TG
Tokelau	NZD	New Zealand Dollar	TK
Tonga	TOP	Pa'anga	TO
Trinidad and Tobago	TTD	Trinidad and Tobago Dollar	TT
Tunisia	TND	Tunisian Dinar	TN
Turkey	TRL	New Turkish Lira	TR
Turkmenistan	TMM	Turkmenistan Manat	TM

Country	Currency Code	Currency	Country Code
Turks and Caicos Islands	USD	US Dollar	TC
Tuvalu	AUD	Australian Dollar	TV
Uganda	UGS	Ugandan Shilling	UG
Ukraine	UAH, UAK, UAG	Hryvnia	UA
United Arab Emirates	AED	UAE Dirham	AE
United Kingdom	GBP (sometimes incorrectly seen as UKP)	Pound Sterling	GB
United States Minor Outlying Islands	USD	US Dollar	UM
United States of America	USD	US Dollar	US
Uruguay	UYU (replacement for UYP)	Uruguayan Peso	UY
Uzbekistan	UZS	Uzbekistani Som (Russian Ruble [RUR] was formerly in use)	UZ
Vanuatu	VUV	Vatu	VU
Venezuela	VEB	Bolivar	VE
Viet Nam	VND	Dông	VN
Virgin Islands (British)	USD (also GBP, XCD)	US Dollar (Pound Sterling and East Caribbean Dollar also circulate)	VG
Virgin Islands (US)	USD	US Dollar	VI

Country	Currency Code	Currency	Country Code
Wallis and Futuna Islands	XPF	Franc des Comptoirs Français du Pacifique	WF
Western Sahara	MAD, MRO	Moroccan Dirham and Mauritanian Ouguiya	EH
Yemen (unified North and South)	YER	Riyal (Dinar was used in South Yemen)	YE (formerly YE for North Yemen and YD for South Yemen)
Zambia	ZMK	Zambian Kwacha	ZM
Zimbabwe	ZWD	Zimbabwe Dollar	ZW

APPENDIX B: FUTURES COMMISSION MERCHANTS (FCMS)

FCMs are required to file monthly financial reports with the Division of Clearing and Intermediary Oversight, a division of the Commodity Futures Trading Commission (CFTC). Reports are required to be filed within 17 business days after the end of the month. The most recent information is usually added within 12 business days after FCMs file their reports, but it could be added later. Once information is posted, it is not revised to reflect any amended data received from a FCM.

The information provided in the table below is a subset of data compiled for 174 FCMs that filed required reports for the month ending October 2006.

CFTC Listing of Futures Commission Merchants (Reporting October 2006)

	Futures Commission Merchant	Registered with the Securities Exchange Commission	Designated Self-Regulatory Organization
1	3D Forex, LLC	N	NFA
2	ABBEY NATIONAL SECURITIES INC	Y	NFA
3	ABN AMRO INCORPORATED	Y	CBOT
4	ADM INVESTOR SERVICES INC	N	CBOT
5	ADVANCED MARKETS INC	N	NFA
6	ADVANTAGE FUTURES LLC	N	CME
7	AG EDWARDS & SONS INC	Y	CBOT
8	AIG CLEARING CORPORATION	N	NYME
9	ALARON TRADING CORPORATION	N	CME
10	ALLIANZ GLOBAL INVESTORS DISTRIBUTORS LLC	Y	NFA
11	ALPHA FOREIGN EXCHANGE GROUP LLC	N	NFA

	Futures Commission Merchant	Registered with the Securities Exchange Commission	Designated Self-Regulatory Organization
12	AMERICAN NATIONAL TRADING CORP	N	NFA
13	BACERA CORPORATION	N	NFA
14	BANC OF AMERICA SECURITIES LLC	Y	CME
15	BARCLAYS CAPITAL INC	Y	NYME
16	BATTERY ASSET MANAGEMENT LLC	N	NFA
17	BEAR STEARNS & CO INC	Y	NFA
18	BEAR STEARNS SECURITIES CORP	Y	CME
19	BNP PARIBAS COMMODITY FUTURES INC	N	NYME
20	BNP PARIBAS SECURITIES CORP	Y	CBOT
21	BROOKSTREET SECURITIES CORPORATION	Y	NFA
22	C CZARNIKOW SUGAR FUTURES INC	N	NFA
23	CADENT FINANCIAL SERVICES LLC	N	CME
24	CAL FINANCIAL CORPORATION	N	NFA
25	CALYON FINANCIAL INC	Y	CME
26	CANTOR FITZGERALD & CO	Y	CBOT
27	CAPITAL MARKET SERVICES LLC	N	NFA
28	CIBC WORLD MARKETS CORP	Y	CME
29	CITIGROUP GLOBAL MARKETS INC	Y	CBOT
30	CLIFF LARSON COMPANY THE	N	NFA
31	CMC MARKETS (US) LLC	N	NFA
32	COMTRUST INC	N	NFA
33	COUNTRY HEDGING INC	N	NFA
34	CREDIT SUISSE SECURITIES (USA) LLC	Y	CBOT
35	CROSSLAND LLC	N	CBOT

	Futures Commission Merchant	Registered with the Securities Exchange Commission	Designated Self-Regulatory Organization
36	CUNNINGHAM COMMODITIES LLC	N	CBOT
37	DAIWA SECURITIES AMERICA INC	Y	CME
38	DEUTSCHE BANK SECURITIES INC	Y	CBOT
39	DIRECT FOREX LLC	N	NFA
40	DORMAN TRADING LLC	N	CME
41	DUNAVANT COMMODITY CORP	N	NYBT
42	E FX OPTIONS LLC	N	NFA
43	EAGLE MARKET MAKERS INC	N	CBOT
44	ED & F MAN COMMODITY ADVISORS INC	N	NFA
45	ELECTRONIC BROKERAGE SYSTEMS LLC	Y	NFA
46	ENSKILDA FUTURES LTD	N	CME
47	FARR FINANCIAL INC	N	NFA
48	FC STONE LLC	N	CME
49	FCT GROUP LLC	N	CME
50	FIMAT PREFERRED LLC	Y	NFA
51	FIMAT USA LLC	Y	NYME
52	FIRST CAPITOL GROUP LLC	N	NFA
53	FOREFRONT INVESTMENTS CORPORATION	N	NFA
54	FOREX CAPITAL MARKETS LLC	N	NFA
55	FOREX CLUB FINANCIAL COMPANY INC	N	NFA
56	FOREX INTERNATIONAL INVESTMENTS INC	N	NFA
57	FOREX LIQUIDITY LLC	N	NFA
58	FORTIS CLEARING AMERICAS LLC	Y	CBOT
59	FORWARD FOREX INC	N	NFA

	Futures Commission Merchant	Registered with the Securities Exchange Commission	Designated Self-Regulatory Organization
60	FREEDOM FX LLC	N	NFA
61	FRIEDBERG MERCANTILE GROUP INC	N	NFA
62	FRONTIER FUTURES INC	N	NFA
63	FUTURES TECH LLC	N	NFA
64	FX OPTION1 INC	N	NFA
65	FX SOLUTIONS LLC	N	NFA
66	FXCM LLC	N	NFA
67	GAIN CAPITAL GROUP LLC	N	NFA
68	GELBER GROUP LLC	N	CBOT
69	GFS FOREX & FUTURES INC	N	NFA
70	GILDER GAGNON HOWE & CO LLC	Y	NFA
71	GLOBAL FUTURES & FOREX LIMITED	Y	CFTC
72	GLOBAL FUTURES LLC	N	NFA
73	GOLDENBERG HEHMEYER & CO	Y	CBOT
74	GOLDMAN SACHS & CO	Y	CBOT
75	GOLDMAN SACHS EXECUTION & CLEARING LP	Y	CME
76	GREENWICH CAPITAL MARKETS INC	Y	CBOT
77	H & R BLOCK FINANCIAL ADVISORS INC	Y	NFA
78	HAGERTY GRAIN CO INC	N	CBOT
79	HAMILTON WILLIAMS LLC	N	NFA
80	HOTSPOT FXR LLC	N	NFA
81	HSBC SECURITIES USA INC	Y	CME
82	I TRADE FX LLC	N	NFA
83	ICAP FUTURES LLC	N	CME

	Futures Commission Merchant	Registered with the Securities Exchange Commission	Designated Self-Regulatory Organization
84	IFSCL USA INC	N	NFA
85	IFX MARKETS INC	N	NFA
86	IG FINANCIAL MARKETS INC.	N	NFA
87	INTEGRATED BROKERAGE SERVICES LLC	N	NFA
88	INTERACTIVE BROKERS LLC	Y	EUXUS
89	INTERBANK FX LLC	N	NFA
90	IOWA GRAIN CO	N	CBOT
91	ITAU SECURITIES INC	Y	NFA
92	IXIS SECURITIES NORTH AMERICA INC	Y	NFA
93	JP MORGAN FUTURES INC	N	NYME
94	KOTTKE ASSOCIATES LLC	N	CBOT
95	LADENBURG THALMANN & CO INC	Y	NFA
96	LBS LIMITED PARTNERSHIP	N	CBOT
97	LEHMAN BROTHERS INC	Y	CBOT
98	LINN GROUP (THE)	N	NFA
99	LINSCO PRIVATE LEDGER CORP	Y	NFA
100	LOEB PARTNERS CORPORATION	Y	NFA
101	MACQUARIE FUTURES USA INC	N	NFA
102	MAN FINANCIAL INC	N	CME
103	MANCHESTER FINANCIAL GROUP INC	N	NFA
104	MARQUETTE ELECTRONIC BROKERAGE LLC	N	NFA
105	MB TRADING FUTURES INC.	N	NFA
106	MBF CLEARING CORP	N	NYME
107	MCVEAN TRADING AND INVESTMENTS LLC	N	NFA

	Futures Commission Merchant	Registered with the Securities Exchange Commission	Designated Self-Regulatory Organization
108	MERRILL LYNCH PIERCE FENNER & SMITH	Y	CBOT
109	MERRILL LYNCH PROFESSIONAL CLEARING CORP	Y	NFA
110	MID-CO COMMODITIES INC	N	NFA
111	MITSUI BUSSAN COMMODITIES USA INC	N	NYME
112	MIZUHO SECURITIES USA INC	Y	CME
113	MONEY GARDEN CORP	N	NFA
114	MORGAN KEEGAN & COMPANY INC	Y	NFA
115	MORGAN STANLEY & CO INCORPORATED	Y	CME
116	MORGAN STANLEY DW INC	Y	CBOT
117	NATIONS INVESTMENTS LLC	N	NFA
118	NEUBERGER BERMAN LLC	Y	NFA
119	NOMURA SECURITIES INTERNATIONAL INC	Y	CBOT
120	OANDA CORPORATION	N	NFA
121	ODL SECURITIES INC	N	NFA
122	ONE WORLD CAPITAL GROUP	N	NFA
123	OPEN E CRY LLC	N	NFA
124	OPPENHEIMER & CO INC	Y	NFA
125	OPTIONSXPRESS INC	Y	NFA
126	PENSON FINANCIAL FUTURES INC	N	NFA
127	PEREGRINE FINANCIAL GROUP INC	N	NFA
128	PIONEER FUTURES INC	N	NYME
129	PIPER JAFFRAY & CO	Y	NFA
130	PRUDENTIAL FINANCIAL DERIVATIVES LLC	N	CBOT

	Futures Commission Merchant	Registered with the Securities Exchange Commission	Designated Self-Regulatory Organization
131	RAND FINANCIAL SERVICES INC	N	CME
132	RAYMOND JAMES & ASSOCIATES INC	Y	NFA
133	RBC CAPITAL MARKETS CORPORATION	Y	CME
134	RBC DAIN RAUSCHER INC	Y	NFA
135	REDSKY FINANCIAL LLC	Y	NFA
136	RJ OBRIEN ASSOCIATES INC	N	CME
137	ROBBINS FUTURES INC	N	NFA
138	ROSENTHAL COLLINS GROUP LLC	N	CME
139	ROSENTHAL GLOBAL SECURITIES LLC	Y	CBOT
140	SANFORD C BERNSTEIN & CO LLC	Y	NFA
141	SENTINEL MANAGEMENT GROUP INC	N	NFA
142	SHATKIN ARBOR INC	N	CBOT
143	SHAY GRAIN CLEARING COMPANY	N	KCBT
144	SMW TRADING COMPANY INC	N	CME
145	SNC INVESTMENTS INC	N	NFA
146	SOLID GOLD FINANCIAL SERVICES INC	N	NFA
147	SPOT FX CLEARING CORP	N	NFA
148	STEPHENS INC	Y	NFA
149	STERLING COMMODITIES CORP	N	NYME
150	TCA FUTURES LLC	N	NFA
151	TENCO INC	N	CBOT
152	TERRA NOVA TRADING LLC	Y	NFA
153	TIMBER HILL LLC	Y	CME
154	TOWER RESEARCH CAPITAL EUROPE LLC	N	NFA
155	TRADELINK LLC	Y	CBOT
156	TRADEMAVEN CLEARING LLC	N	NFA
157	TRADESTATION SECURITIES INC	Y	NFA

	Futures Commission Merchant	Registered with the Securities Exchange Commission	Designated Self-Regulatory Organization
158	TRADITION SECURITIES AND FUTURES INC	N	NFA
159	TRANSMARKET GROUP LLC	Y	CBOT
160	TREND COMMODITIES LIMITED PARTNERSHIP	N	NFA
161	TRILAND USA INC	N	NYME
162	UBS CLEARING SERVICES CORPORATION	Y	NFA
163	UBS FINANCIAL SERVICES INC	Y	CBOT
164	UBS SECURITIES LLC	Y	CBOT
165	UNITED GLOBAL MARKETS LLC	N	NFA
166	VELOCITY FUTURES LP	N	NFA
167	VISION LIMITED PARTNERSHIP	N	NFA
168	WACHOVIA CAPITAL MARKETS LLC	Y	CME
169	WACHOVIA SECURITIES FINANCIAL NETWORK, LLC	Y	NFA
170	WACHOVIA SECURITIES LLC	Y	NFA
171	WALL STREET DERIVATIVES INC	N	NFA
172	WHITE COMMERCIAL CORPORATION	N	NFA
173	XPRESSTRADE LLC	N	NFA
174	YORK BUSINESS ASSOCIATES LLC	N	NFA

NFA -National Futures Association

CBOT - Chicago Board of Trade

CME - Chicago Mercantile Exchange

NYME - New York Mercantile Exchange

APPENDIX C: U.S. FOREX BROKERS

This listing of U.S. Forex broker firms was compiled from the global listing of brokers provided at **http://www.Forex-brokers-list.com**. This Web site includes a moderated listing of Forex brokers. The site guarantees that listed companies provided accurate information about their companies and their company's services at the time data were entered into the listing. Brokers in other nations can also be found at the Web site.

Company title:	AlaronFX Inc.
AlaronFX was launched in June 2001 to offer internet-based foreign-exchange dealing to institutional investors, money managers, and private investors. The company mission is to raise the bar for online Forex trading by offering a professional, technologically superior service that allows small to medium sized investors access to 24-hour, commission-free Forex trading at Interbank spreads. Offered services are ideal for investors who wish to speculate on the direction of the currency markets for profit, as well as money managers or corporate treasurers looking to hedge against unwanted exposure to fluctuations in the currency market.	
Services:	Forex, Managed Forex Accounts, Futures, Options, Managed Funds, News & Analysis, Education
Languages:	English
Trading platform:	Alaron Forex Trader
Commissions on Forex:	no
Bid/Ask spread on Major currencies:	3–5 pips
Maximum Leverage:	100:1

Free Demo Account:	Yes
Mini Forex Trading:	Yes
Contact info	
Address:	AlaronFX Inc. 822 W. Washington Blvd, Chicago IL 60607
Country:	USA
Toll Free:	1-800-613-4402 (within North America)
Int'l:	+01-312-563-8000
Fax number:	312-563-8526
E-mail:	**alaronfx@alaron.com**
Company URL:	**www.alaronfx.com**

Company title:	Forex System Brokers
Address:	25585 Mainsail Way
City:	Dana Point CA
Country:	U.S. & Canada
Zip code:	92629
Telephone number:	949-388-5838
Fax number:	714-242-1653
Company URL:	**www.Forexsystembroker.com**
Services:	Forex
Languages:	English
Trading platform:	
Commissions on Forex:	
Bid/Ask spread on Major currencies:	Pips
Minimal Transaction Size:	0 USD
Minimal Deposit Size:	0 USD

Free Demo Account:	
Mini Forex Trading:	

Company title:	FlashForex.com
Address:	822 West Washington Boulevard Chicago IL
Country:	U.S. & Canada
Zip code:	60607
Telephone number:	800-929-5600
Telephone number:	312-563-8140
Fax number:	312-563-8593
Company URL:	www.FlashForex.com
Services:	Forex
Languages:	English
Trading platform:	Flash Forex
Commissions on Forex:	no
Bid/Ask spread on Major currencies:	Pips
Minimal Transaction Size:	0 USD
Minimal Deposit Size:	1,000 USD
Free Demo Account:	no
Mini Forex Trading:	no

Company title:	COESfx Clearing, Inc
Services:	Forex, Stocks, Stocks on Margin (CFDs), Futures and Fixed Income Products.

Currency pairs are available for trading:	EUR/USD	(Euro Dollar versus U.S. Dollar)
	AUD/USD	(Australian Dollar versus U.S. Dollar)
	EUR/JPY	(Euro Dollar versus Japanese Yen)
	USD/JPY	(U.S. Dollar versus Japanese Yen)
	USD/CHF	(U.S. Dollar versus Swiss Franc)
Currency pairs are available for trading: *(continue)*	USD/CAD	(U.S. Dollar versus Canadian Dollar)
	EUR/CHF	(Euro Dollar versus Swiss Franc)
	GBP/USD	(British Pound versus U.S. Dollar)
	GBP/JPY	(British Pound versus Japanese Yen)
	NZD/USD	(New Zealand Dollar versus U.S. Dollar)
	EUR/GBP	(Euro Dollar versus British Pound)
	EUR/CAD	(Euro Dollar versus Canadian Dollar)
	EUR/AUD	(Euro Dollar versus Australian Dollar)
	AUD/CAD	(Australian Dollar versus Canadian Dollar)
	GBP/AUD	(British Pound versus Australian Dollar
	GBP/CHF	(British pound versus Swiss Franc)
	CHF/JPY	(Swiss Franc versus Japanese Yen)
	CAD/JPY	(Canadian Dollar versus Japanese Yen)
	AUD/JPY	(Australian Dollar versus Japanese Yen)
	AUD/CHF	(Australian Dollar versus Swiss franc)
Commissions on Forex:	No	
Bid/Ask spread on Major currencies:	2–3 pips	

Maximal Leverage:	50 : 1
Minimum account size for Regular Account:	$5,000 MOVE $5,000 1/2 LINE BELOW
Minimum trade:	100,000 US D
Free Demo Account:	yes
Trading platform:	COES Level 1™ Trading Platform Charts can be obtained through COESfx partners at Aspen Graphics. They offer a very robust and comprehensive charting package for traders on all levels.
Regulated:	COESfx was formed and is based in the U.S. and adheres strictly to NFA Regulations. COESfx, Inc., and or COESfx Clearing, Inc., at its sole discretion, reserves the right to terminate an account at any time for non-compliance to the rules and regulations set forth by the NFA. COESfx Clearing, Inc.,© registered with the National Futures Association (NFA ID# 0314715) and CFTC.
Contact info	
Address:	COESfx Clearing, Inc 255 Executive Dr Suite 408 Plainview NY 11803
Country:	U.S.
Toll Free Telephone (US only):	866-430-COES (866-430-2637)

International Telephone:	516-349-9100
Fax number:	516-349-9129
Company URL:	**www.coesfx.com**

Company title:	ProEdge FX
Address:	One South Wacker Drive
City:	Chicago IL
Country:	U.S. & Canada
Zip code:	60606
Telephone number:	800-241-0949
Telephone number:	312-373-6222
Fax number:	312-373-6256
Company URL:	**www.proedgefx.com**
Services:	Forex
Languages:	English, Chinese (simplified)
Trading platform:	
Commissions on Forex:	no
Bid/Ask spread on Major currencies:	3-5 pips
Minimal Transaction Size:	0 USD
Minimal Deposit Size:	0 USD
Free Demo Account:	yes
Mini Forex Trading:	yes

Company title:	Axis Trading Company
Address:	5900 Wilshire Blvd Suite 2535
City:	Los Angeles CA

Country:	U.S. & Canada
Zip code:	90036
Telephone number:	888-998-8880
Telephone number:	323-525-1980
Fax number:	323-525-1479
Company URL:	**www.axistrader.com**
Services:	Forex, Futures, Stocks
Languages:	English
Trading platform:	
Commissions on Forex:	no
Minimal Transaction Size:	0 USD
Minimal Deposit Size:	1,000 USD
Free Demo Account:	yes
Mini Forex Trading:	no

Company title:	ApexForex.com
Address:	One South Wacker Drive, #3875
City:	Chicago IL
Country:	U.S. & Canada
Zip code:	60606
Telephone number:	800-634-9466
Telephone number:	312-373-6251
Company URL:	**www.ApexForex.com**
Services:	Forex, Futures, Options, Managed Funds, News & Analysis, Education
Languages:	English
Trading platform:	Global Trading System

Commissions on Forex:	no
Bid/Ask spread on Major currencies:	3 pips
Minimal Transaction Size:	1,000 USD
Minimal Deposit Size:	500 USD
Free Demo Account:	yes
Mini Forex Trading:	yes
Craig Ross	
Position:	Owner

Company title:	**Global Forex LLC**
Address:	PO Box 6263
City:	North Logan UT
Country:	U.S. & Canada
Zip code:	84341
Telephone number:	435-563-0057
Company URL:	**www.Forexonline.com**
Services:	Forex
Languages:	Russian, English, Spanish, Chinese (simplified), Japanese, Armenian, French, Korean, Romanian
Trading platform:	
Commissions on Forex:	no
Bid/Ask spread on Major currencies:	4-5 pips
Minimal Transaction Size:	500 USD
Minimal Deposit Size:	2,000 USD

Free Demo Account:	yes
Mini Forex Trading:	yes
Steve Hoggan	
Position:	President

Company title:	FX Solutions
Address:	127 East Ridgewood Ave Suite 201
City:	Ridgewood NJ
Country:	U.S. & Canada
Zip code:	07450
Telephone number:	1-201-345-2210
E-mail:	send message
Company URL:	**www.fxsol.com**
Services:	Forex, Managed Funds
Languages:	English, Chinese (simplified), Chinese (traditional)
Trading platform:	Global Trading System
Commissions on Forex:	no
Bid/Ask spread on Major currencies:	3–4 pips
Minimal Transaction Size:	10 USD
Minimal Deposit Size:	300 USD
Free Demo Account:	yes
Mini Forex Trading:	yes
Thomas Plaut	
Position:	Managing Partner

Company title:	IFX Markets Inc.
Address:	20 Park Plaza Suite 612
City:	Boston MA
Country:	U.S. & Canada
Zip code:	02116
Telephone number:	617-357-0682
Fax number:	617-357-0055
Company URL:	**www.cbfx.com**
Services:	Forex
Languages:	Russian, English, Spanish, Polish
Trading platform:	CBFX Online
Commissions on Forex:	no
Bid/Ask spread on Major currencies:	3–5 pips
Minimal Transaction Size:	10 USD
Minimal Deposit Size:	500 USD
Free Demo Account:	yes
Mini Forex Trading:	yes
Ryan Nettles	
Position:	Director of Sales
Telephone number:	617-357-0682
Fax:	617-357-0055

Company title:	Alipes Forex Trading Services
Address:	P.O. Box 1332
City:	Burbank CA
Country:	U.S.
Zip code:	91510

Telephone number:	626-644-7883
Company URL:	**http://www.alipes.net**
Services:	Forex, Managed Funds, News & Analysis
Languages:	Russian, English, Polish, Arabic, French, German
Trading platform:	
Commissions on Forex:	no
Bid/Ask spread on Major currencies:	3–5 pips
Minimal Transaction Size:	20,000 USD
Minimal Deposit Size:	2,000 USD
Free Demo Account:	yes
Mini Forex Trading:	yes
USA	
Position:	-
Telephone number:	626-644-7883
Fax:	818-848-9359
Switzerland	
Position:	
Telephone number:	412-279-70338
Fax:	412-279-62146

Company title:	**Alipes Forex Trading Services**
Address:	P.O. Box 1332
City:	Burbank
State / Province:	CA
Country:	USA

Zip code:	91510
Telephone number:	626-644-7883
Company URL:	**http://www.alipes.net**
Services:	Forex, Managed Funds, News & Analysis
Languages:	Russian, English, Polish, Arabic, French, German
Trading platform:	
Commissions on Forex:	no
Bid/Ask spread on Major currencies:	3–5 pips
Minimal Transaction Size:	20,000 USD
Minimal Deposit Size:	2,000 USD
Free Demo Account:	yes
Mini Forex Trading:	yes
Telephone number:	626-644-7883
Fax:	818-848-9359
Switzerland	
Telephone number:	412-279-70338
Fax:	412-279-62146

Company title:	**Capital Market Services, LLC. CMS Forex**

Services:	CMS offers trading using the VT Trader platform where clients can execute orders automatically based on their own trading systems with FX AutoPilot. CMS features exclusive daily, weekly, and monthly commentary by world renowned Forex analyst Hans Nilsson.
Languages:	English, Spanish, German, French, Italian, Portuguese, Chinese, Japanese, Korean, Arabic, Russian, Polish, Taiwanese, Mandarin, Cantonese
Trading platform:	Visual Trading (VT Trader)
Commissions on Forex:	no
Bid/Ask spread on Major currencies:	3–4 pips
Maximum Leverage:	400:1
Minimal Deposit Size:	200 USD
Free Demo Account:	yes
Mini Forex Trading:	yes
Address:	Empire State Building 350 5th Avenue Suite 6400 New York NY 10118
Country:	USA
Telephone number:	212-563-2100
Fax number:	212-563-4994

E-mail:	**customerservice@cmsfx.com**
Company URL:	**www.cmsfx.com**

Company title:	**FXTech Trading**
Address:	100 State Street
City:	Boston
State / Province:	
Country:	U.S. & Canada
Zip code:	MA 02109
Telephone number:	800-511-4685 x101
Fax number:	617-557-9220
Company URL:	**www.fxtrading.com**
Services:	Forex
Languages:	English
Trading platform:	
Commissions on Forex:	no
Bid/Ask spread on Major currencies:	5 pips
Minimal Transaction Size:	100 USD
Minimal Deposit Size:	0 USD
Free Demo Account:	yes
Mini Forex Trading:	no
Michael Dion	
Position:	Principal

Company title:	**Goldberg Forex Group**
Address:	17027 West Dixie Hwy Suite 102
City:	Miami FL

Country:	U.S. & Canada
Zip code:	33160
Telephone number:	305-947-9956
Company URL:	**www.goldbergForex.com**
Services:	Forex
Languages:	Chinese (simplified), English, Spanish
Trading platform:	
Commissions on Forex:	yes
Bid/Ask spread on Major currencies:	5–6 pips
Minimal Transaction Size:	10,000USD
Minimal Deposit Size:	250 USD
Free Demo Account:	yes
Mini Forex Trading:	yes
Carlos Vivas	
Position:	President
Telephone number:	305-947-9956

Company title:	**Rose Stevens & Company**
Address:	59 North Main St
City:	Florida NY
Country:	U.S. & Canada
Zip code:	10921
Telephone number:	845-651-4300
Company URL:	**www.RoseStevens.com**
Services:	Managed Funds
Languages:	English

Trading platform:	
Commissions on Forex:	no
Bid/Ask spread on Major currencies:	0 pips
Minimal Transaction Size:	0 USD
Minimal Deposit Size:	50,000 USD
Free Demo Account:	no
Mini Forex Trading:	no
Peter Rosenstreich	
Position:	Trader

Company title:	**DirectFX**
Address:	141 W Jackson Suite 1220
City:	Chicago IL
Country:	U.S. & Canada
Zip code:	60604
Telephone number:	312-294-8109
Company URL:	**www.directfx.com**
Services:	Forex
Languages:	English
Trading platform:	Global Trading System
Commissions on Forex:	no
Bid/Ask spread on Major currencies:	3–5 pips
Minimal Transaction Size:	1,000 USD
Minimal Deposit Size:	200 USD
Free Demo Account:	yes
Mini Forex Trading:	yes

Glenn Kaihara	
Position:	VP

Company title:	DTG Futures
Address:	141 W Jackson Suite 1220
City:	Chicago IL
Country:	U.S. & Canada
Zip code:	60604
Telephone number:	312-294-8109
Company URL:	**www.dtgfutures.com**
Services:	Futures
Languages:	English
Trading platform:	J-Trader, Ran Order Pro, Ran Order Basic
Commissions on Forex:	no
Bid/Ask spread on Major currencies:	0 pips
Minimal Transaction Size:	0 USD
Minimal Deposit Size:	0 USD
Free Demo Account:	yes
Mini Forex Trading:	no
Glenn Kaihara	
Position:	VP

Company title:	Forex.com
Address:	35 Technology Drive
City:	Warren NJ
Country:	U.S. & Canada

Zip code:	07059
Telephone number:	908-731-0750
Telephone number:	877-ForexGO
Fax number:	908-731-0701
Company URL:	**www.Forex.com**
Services:	Forex
Languages:	Chinese (simplified), Chinese (traditional), English
Trading platform:	
Commissions on Forex:	yes
Bid/Ask spread on Major currencies:	4–5 pips
Minimal Transaction Size:	10 USD
Minimal Deposit Size:	250 USD
Free Demo Account:	yes
Mini Forex Trading:	yes
Client Relations Department	
Position:	Client Relations
Telephone number:	1-908-731-0750
Fax:	1-908-731-0701

Company title:	**MVP Global Forex, LLC**
Address:	15 Park Row Floor 23
City:	New York NY
Country:	U.S. & Canada
Zip code:	10038
Telephone number:	212-962-2100
Telephone number:	877-962-2100

Fax number:	212-898-0158
Company URL:	**www.MVPGlobalForex.com**
Services:	Forex, Futures, Managed Funds, Education
Languages:	English, Chinese (simplified), Chinese (traditional)
Trading platform:	Global Trading System, J-Trader, Global Trading System (GTS)
Commissions on Forex:	no
Bid/Ask spread on Major currencies:	3-4 pips
Minimal Transaction Size:	1,000 USD
Minimal Deposit Size:	500 USD
Free Demo Account:	yes
Mini Forex Trading:	yes
Robert Mendelow	
Position:	Managing Director
Telephone number:	877-962-2100
Fax:	212-898-0158

Company title:	**Gallo Global Markets**
Address:	875 N Michigan Ave Suite 1562
City:	Chicago IL
Country:	U.S. & Canada
Zip code:	60611
Telephone number:	+1-312-274-3413
Fax number:	+1-312-274-3405
Company URL:	**www.ggmk.com**

Services:	Forex, Futures, Options, Managed Funds, News & Analysis, Education
Languages:	English, French, German, Hebrew, Italian, Portuguese, Slovak
Trading platform:	Global Trading System, Microsoft, J-Trader
Commissions on Forex:	no
Bid/Ask spread on Major currencies:	3 pips
Minimal Transaction Size:	50,000 USD
Minimal Deposit Size:	300 USD
Free Demo Account:	yes
Mini Forex Trading:	yes
Marco Bertuglia	
Position:	Managing Director
Telephone number:	+1-312-274-3413
Fax:	+1-312-274-3405
Carlo Scevola	
Position:	Chairman

Company title:	Forex For You
Address:	111 Pine Street #1300
City:	San Francisco
State / Province:	California
Country:	U.S. & Canada
Zip code:	94111
Telephone number:	1-415-433-8888

Telephone number:	1-415-433-8888
Fax number:	1-415-433-8880
Company URL:	**http://www.Forexforyou.com**
Services:	Forex, Managed Funds, Education
Languages:	English
Trading platform:	Openex
Commissions on Forex:	no
Bid/Ask spread on Major currencies:	3-6 pips
Minimal Transaction Size:	0 USD
Minimal Deposit Size:	10 USD
Free Demo Account:	yes
Mini Forex Trading:	no
Wes Gibson	
Position:	Introducing Broker, Professional Currency Trader.
Telephone number:	1-415-433-8888
Fax:	1-415-433-8880

Company title:	**Forex Day Trading**
Address:	2150 SW 22 St
City:	Miami fl
Country:	U.S. & Canada
Zip code:	33145
Telephone number:	786-866-8733
Telephone number:	800-366-4157
Fax number:	786-206-1407

Company URL:	http://www.Forex-day-trading.com
Services:	Forex, Managed Funds, Education
Languages:	English, Spanish
Trading platform:	
Commissions on Forex:	no
Bid/Ask spread on Major currencies:	4–5 pips
Minimal Transaction Size:	10,000 USD
Minimal Deposit Size:	250 USD
Free Demo Account:	yes
Mini Forex Trading:	yes
Forex Support Department	
Position:	Client Support and Training
Telephone number:	786-866-8733
Fax:	786-206-1407

Company title:	**Currency Trading USA**
Address:	2150 SW 22 St
City:	Miami Fl
Country:	USA & Canada
Zip code:	33145
Telephone number:	786-866-8733
Telephone number:	800-366-4157
Fax number:	786-206-1407
Company URL:	**www.currencytradingusa.com**
Services:	Forex, Managed Funds, Education

Languages:	English, Spanish
Trading platform:	
Commissions on Forex:	no
Bid/Ask spread on Major currencies:	4–5 pips
Minimal Transaction Size:	10,000 USD
Minimal Deposit Size:	250 USD
Free Demo Account:	yes
Mini Forex Trading:	yes
Trading Support Department	
Position:	Currency Trading Support and Training
Telephone number:	786-866-8733
Fax:	786-206-1407

Company title:	**A. B. Watley FX, Inc.** Division of ODL Securities Inc.
Services:	Forex, Futures, Stocks, Options, Managed Funds, News & Analysis, Education
Languages:	Chinese (simplified), Danish, English, French, German, Greek, Hebrew, Irish, Italian, Japanese, Korean, Portuguese, Russian, Scottish, Spanish, Swedish, Turkish
Trading platform:	Flash Forex
Commissions on Forex:	no

Bid/Ask spread on Major currencies:	3–5 pips
Maximum Leverage:	100:1
Minimal Deposit Size:	$2,000$ 500 (Mini account)
Free Demo Account:	yes
Mini Forex Trading:	yes
Contact info	
Address:	50 Broad Street Suite 1728
City:	New York NY
Country:	U.S.
Telephone number:	866-4-WATLEY 866-492-8539)
Company URL:	**www.abwatleyfx.com**

Company title:	FXDirectDealer
Address:	75 Park Place, 4th Floor
City:	New York NY
Zip code:	10007
Country:	USA
Toll-free number:	1-866-FOR-FXDD (367-3933)
Main Telephone number:	1-212-791-FXDD (3933)
Fax number:	1-212-937-3845
E-mail:	**sales@fxdd.com**
Company URL:	**www.fxdd.com**
Services:	Forex
Languages:	English, Chinese Simple, Korean
Trading platform:	FXDD Trader, MetaTrader

Commissions on Forex:	no
Bid/Ask spread on Major currencies:	3-5 pips
Quoted Currencies:	19 currency pairs EUR/USD, USD/JPY, GBP/USD, USD/CHF, EUR/JPY, EUR/GBP, GBP/JPY, EUR/CHF, USD/CAD, AUD/USD, CHF/JPY, GBP/CHF, EUR/AUD, EUR/CAD, AUD/CAD, AUD/JPY, AUD/NZD, NZD/USD, USD/MXN.
Maximum Leverage:	100:1 for a regular account 200:1 for a mini account
Mini Forex Trading:	yes
Free Demo Account:	yes
Trading Desk	
Toll-free number:	1-866-FOR-FXDD (367-3933)
Main Telephone number:	1-212-791-FXDD (3933)
Fax number:	1-212-937-3845
E-mail:	**tradingdesk@fxdd.com**

APPENDIX D: DISCIPLINED FINANCIAL FIRMS

The following is an alphabetical list of financial firms that have been disciplined for Sale Practice Fraud. A disciplined firm has been formally charged by the CFTC or NFA with deceptive telemarketing practices or promotional material. The firm has been permanently barred from the industry as a result of the charges. The listing also includes the NFA ID of each firm, which links to more specific information relative to the fraud and disciplinary actions as well as the date the firm was added to the listing.

Firms Disciplined for Sales Practice Fraud		
Firm Name	NFA ID	Date added to list
1ST COMMODITY CORP OF THE CAROLINAS	0203487	6/17/1999
618 INVESTMENT GROUP INC	0239211	6/1/2001
AFFILIATED SECURITY BROKERS	0086381	6/1/2001
ALEXIS FINANCIAL GROUP INC	0244775	2/17/2000
ALPINE FINANCIAL CORP	0251031	9/18/1999
AMERICAN FINANCIAL GROUP SERVICES INC	0275199	7/13/2000
AMERICAN FINANCIAL TRADING CORP	0267144	10/12/2005
AMERICAN FIRST FINANCIAL INVESTMENT CORP	0222283	6/1/2001
AMERICAN FUTURES GROUP INC	0089434	5/19/1998
APACHE TRADING CORPORATION	0000649	12/5/1994
ARBITRAGE SERVICES CORPORATION	0002878	6/1/2001

ARNEKAY INC	0002768	12/5/1994
ATLANTIC FUTURES INC	0002516	12/5/1994
ATLANTIC MERCANTILE GROUP INC	0219013	12/5/1994
B P FINANCIAL OF BOSTON INC	0186609	12/5/1994
BACHUS & STRATTON COMMODITIES INC	0197022	12/5/1994
BAXTER INVESTMENTS INC	0205337	6/1/2001
BAY LIMITED	0226102	6/1/2001
BEAR & WOLF COMPANY INC	0271239	1/25/1999
BENTLEY TRADING GROUP INC	0321531	10/27/2006
CALIBER FINANCIAL GROUP LTD	0002103	6/1/2001
CALVARY FINANCIAL GROUP LLC	0297789	4/1/2003
CAPITAL OPTIONS INVESTMENTS INCORPORATED	0199039	6/1/2001
CARHARTT L P AND COMPANY INC	0192585	6/1/2001
CARRINGTON FINANCIAL CORP	0240380	10/2/1997
CASTLE COMMODITIES CORPORATION	0217352	6/1/2001
CENTURY TRADING GROUP INC	0293880	6/1/2001
CERES TRADING GROUP INC	0262793	6/1/2001
CHASE COMMODITIES CORP	0326799	10/18/2006
CHICAGO COMMODITY CORP	0086366	12/5/1994
CHILMARK COMMODITIES CORP	0177592	12/5/1994
CHURCHILL GROUP INC	0211644	12/5/1994
COMMODITY CONSULTANTS INTERNATIONAL INC	0310036	10/12/2005
COMMODITY FLUCTUATIONS SYSTEMS INC	0001201	12/5/1994

COMMONWEALTH FINANCIAL GROUP INC	0238065	5/5/1997
CONCORDE TRADING GROUP INC	0210383	7/1/2002
COUNTRYWIDE TRADING CORPORATION	0330974	11/24/2006
CRESTWOOD CAPITAL MANAGEMENT INC	0000551	6/1/2001
CROMWELL FINANCIAL SERVICES INC	0245020	11/24/2006
DE JONES COMMODITIES INC	0002586	12/5/1994
DING ERIK	0264368	6/1/2001
DIVERSIFIED TRADING SYSTEMS INC	0219677	12/5/1994
DM MCKENZIE AND ASSOCIATES INC	0215215	6/1/2001
DUNHILL FINANCIAL GROUP INC	0266146	3/16/2000
DUNHILL INVESTMENTS CORPORATION	0212041	12/5/1994
DURKIN & ASSOCIATES INC	0089950	12/5/1994
E DAVID STEPHENS COMMODITIES CORP	0086898	12/5/1994
EINSTEIN CISVEST INC	0194816	6/1/2001
ENGLAND MARK W	0176201	12/5/1994
EXECUTIVE COMMODITY CORP	0292976	7/6/2006
FIDELITY MERCANTILE CORP	0259211	9/1/2001
FINANCIAL MEDIA DISTRIBUTION INC	0287990	10/12/2005
FINANCIAL SERVICES GROUP INC	0183300	12/5/1994
FIRST COMMODITY CORP OF BOSTON	0002574	12/5/1994
FIRST INTERNATIONAL COMMODITY GROUP INC	0294760	8/8/2005
FIRST INVESTORS GRP OF PALM BEACHES INC	0246772	11/16/2004

FIRST NATIONAL MONETARY CORP	0001520	12/5/1994
FIRST SIERRA CORPORATION	0205421	12/5/1994
FSG INTERNATIONAL INCORPORATED	0202011	4/2/2001
FUTURES FINANCIAL ADVISORS OF PALM BEACH	0190587	12/5/1994
FUTURES FIRST OF ARIZONA INC	0195792	6/1/2001
FUTURES TRADING GROUP INC	0245339	6/1/2001
FUTUREWISE TRADING GROUP INC	0292458	10/12/2005
GABRIEL BROKERAGE INC	0001779	12/5/1994
GEMINI INVESTMENTS INC	0222892	12/5/1994
GLOBAL TELECOM INC	0284737	11/28/2005
GRANDVIEW HOLDING CORP	0090133	6/1/1996
GREAT AMERICAN COMMODITIES INC	0190158	12/5/1994
HARRINGTON FINANCIAL & ENERGY ADVISORS	0312640	7/6/2006
HARTFORD FINANCIAL GROUP INC	0275227	6/1/2001
HAWAII INVESTMENT NETWORK	0229904	6/1/2001
HVM HOLDINGS INC	0287376	10/12/2005
INDEX SERVICES INC	0000563	12/5/1994
INDUSTRIAL INVESTMENTS CORPORATION	0218142	6/1/2001
INFINITY TRADING CO INC	0234700	6/1/2001
INTERNATIONAL COMMODITIES CORP CHICAGO	0184691	6/1/2001
INTERNATIONAL FUTURES STRATEGISTS INC	0192218	12/5/1994
INTERNATIONAL TRADING GROUP LTD	0002912	12/5/1994

INVESTMENT SYNDICATION CORPORATION	0086844	12/5/1994
INVESTOR ONE FINANCIAL CORP	0307479	5/19/2006
JCC INC	0001612	2/5/1994
LAKE DOW CAPITAL LLC	0320066	5/26/2006
LLOYD ALEXANDER FUTURES LTD	0210246	6/1/2001
LLOYD STEVENS & CO INC	0257918	6/1/2001
LYNCH & COMPANY LLC	0256371	4/1/2003
MADISON FINANCIAL GROUP LLC	0287038	12/1/2003
MASTERS TRADING ORGANIZATION LTD	0087140	12/5/1994
MBH COMMODITY ADVISORS INC	0001782	6/1/2001
MCDINE & ASSOCIATES INC	0223905	6/1/2001
MCKERR JAMES T	0000536	6/1/2001
MIZNER FINANCIAL TRADING CORP	0346896	10/27/2006
MONTGOMERY INTERNATIONAL TRADING INC	0002575	12/5/1994
MULTIVEST OPTIONS INC	0001646	12/5/1994
MURLAS COMMODITIES INC	0002806	12/5/1994
NATIONWIDE FUTURES CORPORATION	0088755	12/5/1994
NEIMANN LLOYDS INC	0002826	12/5/1994
NEMITOFF COMMODITIES CORP	0001913	6/1/2001
NEW FOREST CAPITAL MANAGEMENT INC	0237798	6/1/2001
NORTHWEST FUTURES MANAGEMENT INC	0085961	6/1/2001
OPTION AMERICA INC	0196928	12/5/1994
OPTION STRATEGIES LTD	0000184	6/1/2001
OPTIONS ADVISORY GROUP	0215060	6/1/2001

PAYCHER ABRAHAM	0000435	6/1/2001
PORTER SMITH & CO INC	0281474	8/19/1999
PREFERRED COMMODITY CORPORATION	0217518	11/20/1996
PREMEX INCORPORATED	0000805	12/5/1994
PRESIDENTIAL FUTURES INC	0196723	12/5/1994
PROFITEX INC	0192049	6/1/2001
PROFUSION HOLDINGS LLC	0314508	10/12/2005
QUALIFIED LEVERAGE PROVIDERS INC	0337534	11/24/2006
SCHAFFNER ENTERPRISES INC GERRY	0089848	6/1/2001
SCHAFFNER GERALD	0208572	6/1/2001
SCOTT D WOLFE CTA INC	0236622	6/1/2001
SHUN PUN LIMITED	0089769	6/1/2001
SIEGEL TRADING CO INC THE	0001085	2/3/2004
SMITH BAISAL DWIGHT	0254922	6/1/2001
SMITH GEORGE COLE	0000221	6/1/2001
SOUTH COAST COMMODITIES INC	0346902	12/1/2006
STAR COMMODITIES LTD	0236694	6/1/2001
STIRN BARRY GERALD	0090046	12/5/1994
T H D INCORPORATED	0086043	6/1/2001
TARA SECURITIES CORP	0177594	12/5/1994
TE DEUM CORP	0214703	6/1/2001
TERRANOVA FINANCIAL TRADING CORP	0339938	10/27/2006
TRADER SERVICES CO	0271095	6/1/2001
TRINITY FINANCIAL GROUP INC	0231027	12/5/1994
UNITED FINANCIAL TRADING CORP	0297737	4/3/2006
UNITED INVESTORS GROUP	0309217	10/18/2006

UNIVERSAL FINANCIAL HOLDING CORP	0267903	3/16/2005
UNIVERSAL FUTURES INC	0257807	6/1/2001
US OPTIONS CORP	0274665	12/1/2002
VISTA FUTURES INC	0088658	6/1/2001
VUE VENIR ASSOCIATES INC	0183486	6/1/2001
WACHTEL FINANCIAL GROUP	0207947	6/1/2001
WALLSTREET FINANCIAL TRADING INCORPORATED	0334871	4/3/2006
WALTERS WILLIAM G	0090199	6/1/2001
WATERS TAN & CO INC	0180439	12/5/1994
WELLINGTON FINANCIAL GROUP INC	0276332	11/9/1999
WHITEHALL INVESTORS INTERNATIONAL INC	0002437	12/5/1994
WILSHIRE INVESTMENT MANAGEMENT CORP	0280498	10/18/2006
WOLF COMMODITIES CORP INC	0265565	1/25/1999
WORLD TRADING GROUP INC	0088760	6/1/2001
WORLDWIDE COMMODITY CORPORATION	0291471	12/1/2006
ZIPKIN WILLIAM L	0002040	12/5/1994

NFA ID Web Links

The following table shows select portions of the case summary that may be accessed by following the NFA ID link for 1st Commodity Corp of the Carolinas, for example.

Case Summary

1ST COMMODITY CORP OF THE CAROLINAS	NFA 90BCC00013	NFA ID: 0203487

Respondent/Effective Date Summary		
NFA ID	**Respondent**	**Effective Date**
0203487	1ST COMMODITY CORP OF THE CAROLINAS	11/14/1990
0222035	GASS, STEVEN GREGORY	09/21/1990
Penalty/Event Summary		
	Respondent	**Penalty/Event**
0203487	1ST COMMODITY CORP OF THE CAROLINAS	PERMANENT WITHDRAWAL FROM NFA MEMBERSHIP
0222035	GASS, STEVEN GREGORY	PERMANENT BAR FROM NFA MEMBERSHIP

CASE STUDY: STEVEN GREGORY GASS

Complaint

On June 12, 1990, the Eastern Regional Business conduct committee ("eastern committee") issued a complaint against 1st Commodity Corporation of the Carolinas d/b/a First Futures Group ("ffg") and Steven Gregory Gass ("gass"). The complaint alleges that ffg and Gass violated nfa compliance rules 2-2(a),

CASE STUDY: STEVEN GREGORY GASS

2-29(a)(1) and 2-29(a)(2) by cheating, defrauding, or deceiving; or attempting to cheat, defraud, or deceive commodity futures customers and by making communication with the public which operates as a fraud or deceit and which employs or is part of a high-pressure approach. The complaint also alleges that ffg violated nfa compliance rules 2-29(b)(2) and 2-29(b)(3) by using promotional material which omits facts making the promotional material misleading and which mentions the possibility of profit without an equally prominent statement of the risk of loss; violated nfa compliance rule 2-29(e) by failing to maintain a record of the review and approval of promotional material; and violated nfa compliance rule 2-15 by failing to enforce written option procedures. The complaint further alleges that ffg violated nfa compliance rule 2-30(g) by failing to maintain a record of customer information; violated nfa compliance rules 2-19 and 2-26 by failing to obtain a signed acknowledgement of receipt of an option risk disclosure statement or a risk disclosure statement for its accounts; and violated nfa compliance rule 2-10 by failing to maintain adequate records. Finally, the complaint alleges that ffg violated nfa financial requirements section 9 by failing to maintain written authorization for a qualifying bank account and violated nfa registration rule 210(a) by failing to correct a deficiency in its form 7-r.

Decision - Steven Gregory Gass

On September 21, 1990, the Eastern Committee issued a decision in which it permanently barred Gass from association with any nfa member. Gass failed to file an answer to the complaint and, therefore, pursuant to nfa compliance rule 3-5, the Eastern Committee found that Gass admitted the factual allegations and legal conclusions contained in the complaint and that he has waived his right to a hearing in this matter. The Eastern Committee also found, based on the admission of all the allegations, that Gass committed each and every one of the acts, omissions and violations alleged in Count I of the complaint. Specifically, the Eastern Committee found that Gass violated nfa compliance rules 2-2 and 2-29 by misrepresenting the past trading performance of his clients, misrepresenting his level of experience in the commodities industry,

CASE STUDY: STEVEN GREGORY GASS

misrepresenting ffg's trading performance, misrepresenting the nature of the account forms, misrepresenting the worth of ffg's president, and minimizing the risk involved in commodity trading and misrepresenting his ability to protect a customer from trading losses. The Eastern Committee also found that Gass violated nfa compliance rule 2-29 by making sales solicitations, which contained numerous misrepresentations of fact and numerous statements stressing the need to invest right away. The Eastern Committee found that these acts and omissions constitute conduct which is inconsistent with just and equitable principles of trade.

Decision – 1st Commodity Corporation of the Carolinas

D/B/A First Futures Group

On November 14, 1990, the Eastern Committee issued a decision in which it accepted ffg's settlement offer. Ffg neither admitted nor denied the allegations charged in the complaint, but pursuant to its offer, ffg agreed to withdraw permanently from nfa membership.

APPENDIX E: LIST OF CENTRAL BANKS

Albania: Banka e Shqipërisë **www.bankofalbania.org**
Algeria: Banque d'Algerie **www.bank-of-algeria.dz**
Argentina: Banco Central de la República Argentina **www.bcra.gov.ar**
Armenia: Central Bank of Armenia **www.cba.am**
Aruba: Centrale Bank van Aruba **www.cbaruba.org**
Australia: Reserve Bank of Australia **www.rba.gov.au**
Austria: Oesterreichische Nationalbank **www.oenb.at**
Bahrain: Bahrain Monetary Agency **www.bma.gov.bh**
Barbados: Central Bank of Barbados **www.centralbank.org.bb**
Belgium: National Bank of Belgium **www.bnb.be**
Bermuda: Bermuda Monetary Authority **www.bma.bm**
Bolivia: Banco Central de Bolivia **www.bcb.gov.bo**
Bosnia and Herzegovina: Centralna Banka Bosne i Hercegovine **www.cbbh.gov.ba**
Botswana: Bank of Botswana **www.bankofbotswana.bw**
Brazil: Banco Central do Brasil **www.bcb.gov.br**

Bulgaria: Bulgarska Narodna Banka **www.bnb.bg**
Canada: Bank of Canada **http://www.bankofcanada.ca/**
Cape Verde: Banco de Cabo Verde **www.bcv.cv**
Cayman Islands: Cayman Islands Monetary Authority **www.cimoney.com.ky**
Chile: Banco Central de Chile **www.bcentral.cl**
China: Zhongguo Renmin Yinhang **www.pbc.gov.cn**
Colombia: Banco de la República de Colombia **www.banrep.gov.co**
Costa Rica: Banco Central de Costa Rica **www.bccr.fi.cr**
Croatia: Hrvatska Narodna Banka **www.hnb.hr**
Cyprus: Central Bank of Cyprus **www.centralbank.gov.cy**
Czech Republic: Ceska Národní Banka **www.cnb.cz**
Denmark: Danmarks Nationalbank **www.nationalbanken.dk**
Djibouti: Banque Nationale Djibouti **www.banque-centrale.dj**
Dominican Republic: Banco Central de la República Dominicana **www.bancentral.gov.do**
Eastern Caribbean: Eastern Caribbean Central Bank **www.eccb-centralbank.org**
Ecuador: Banco Central del Ecuador **www.bce.fin.ec**

El Salvador: Banco Central de Reserva de El Salvador **www.bcr.gob.sv**
Estonia: Eesti Pank **www.www.ee/epbe**
European Central Bank **http://www.ecb.int/home/html/index.en.html**
Faroe Islands: Landsbanki Føroya **www.landsbank.fo**
Fiji: Reserve Bank of Fiji **www.reservebank.gov.fj**
Finland: Suomen Pankki **www.bof.fi**
France: Banque de France **www.banque-france.fr**
Georgia: National Bank of Georgia **www.nbg.gov.ge**
Germany: Deutsche Bundesbank **www.bundesbank.de**
Greece: Bank of Greece **www.bankofgreece.gr**
Guatemala: Banco de Guatemala **www.banguat.gob.gt**
Guyana: Bank of Guyana **www.bankofguyana.org.gy**
Haiti: Banque de la République d'Haïti **www.brh.net**
Honduras: Banco Central de Honduras **www.bch.hn**
Hong Kong: Hong Kong Monetary Authority **www.info.gov.hk/hkma**
Hungary: Magyar Nemzeti Bank **www.mnb.hu**

Iceland: Seðlabanki Íslands **www.sedlabanki.is**
India: Reserve Bank of India **www.rbi.org.in**
Indonesia: Bank Sentral Republik Indonesia **www.bi.go.id**
Iran: Central Bank of the Islamic Republic of Iran **www.cbi.ir**
Ireland: Central Bank of Ireland **www.centralbank.ie**
Israel: Bank of Israel **www.bankisrael.gov.il**
Italy: Banca d'Italia **www.bancaditalia.it**
Jamaica: Bank of Jamaica **www.boj.org.jm**
Japan: Bank of Japan **www.boj.or.jp**
Jordan: Central Bank of Jordai **www.cbj.gov.jo**
Kazakhstan: Kazakstan Ulttyk Banki **www.nationalbank.kz**
Kenya: Central Bank of Kenya **www.centralbank.go.ke**
Korea, South: Bank of Korea **www.bok.or.kr**
Kuwait: Central Bank of Kuwait **www.cbk.gov.kw**
Latvia: Latvijas Banka **www.bank.lv**
Lebanon: Banque Du Liban **www.bdl.gov.lb**

Lesotho: Central Bank of Lesotho **www.centralbank.org.ls**
Lithuania: Lietuvos Bankas **www.lbank.lt**
Luxembourg: Banque Centrale de Luxembourg **www.bcl.lu**
Macau: Monetary Authority of Macau **www.amcm.macau.gov.mo**
Macedonia, Former Yugoslav Republic of: National Bank of the Republic of Macedonia **www.nbrm.gov.mk**
Malawi: Reserve Bank of Malawi **www.rbm.malawi.net**
Malaysia: Bank Negara Malaysia **www.bnm.gov.my**
Malta: Central Bank of Malta **www.centralbankmalta.com**
Mauritius: Bank of Mauritius **www.bom.intnet.mu**
Mexico: Banco de México **www.banxico.org.mx**
Moldova: Banca Nationala a Moldovei **www.bnm.org/index1.html**
Mozambique: Banco de Moçambique **www.bancomoc.mz**
Namibia: Bank of Namibia **www.bon.com.na**
Nepal: Nepal Rastra Bank **www.nrb.org.np**
Netherlands Antilles: Bank van de Nederlandse Antillen **www.centralbank.an**

Netherlands: Nederlandsche Bank
www.dnb.nl
New Zealand: Reserve Bank of New Zealand
www.rbnz.govt.nz
Nicaragua: Banco Central de Nicaragua
www.bcn.gob.ni
Norway: Norges Bank
www.norges-bank.no
Oman: Central Bank Of Oman
www.cbo-oman.org
Pakistan: State Bank of Pakistan
www.sbp.org.pk
Palestinian Authority: Palestinian Monetary Authority
www.pma-palestine.org
Paraguay: Banco Central del Paraguay
www.bcp.gov.py
Peru: Banco Central de Reserva del Peru
www.bcrp.gob.pe
Philippines: Bangko Sentral ng Pilipinas
www.bsp.gov.ph
Poland: Narodowy Bank Polski
www.nbp.pl
Portugal: Banco de Portugal
www.bportugal.pt
Qatar: Qatar Central Bank
www.qcb.gov.qa
Romania: National Bank of Romania
www.bnro.ro
Russia: Bank of Russia
www.cbr.ru
San Marino: Istituto di Credito Sammarinese
www.ics.sm

Saudi Arabia: Saudi Arabian Monetary Agency **www.sama.gov.sa**
Singapore: Monetary Authority of Singapore **www.mas.gov.sg**
Slovakia: Národná Banka Slovenska **www.nbs.sk**
Slovenia: Banka Slovenije **www.bsi.si**
South Africa: South African Reserve Bank **www.resbank.co.za**
Spain: Banco de España **www.bde.es**
Swaziland: Central Bank of Swaziland **www.centralbank.sz**
Sweden: Sveriges Riksbank **www.riksbank.se**
Switzerland: Schweiserische Nationalbank **www.snb.ch**
Taiwan: Central Bank of China **www.cbc.gov.tw**
Tanzania: Bank of Tanzania **www.bot-tz.org**
Thailand: Bank of Thailand **www.bot.or.th**
Trinidad and Tobago: Central Bank of Trinidad and Tobago **www.central-bank.org.tt**
Tunisia: Banque Centrale de Tunisie **www.bct.gov.tn**
Turkey: Türkiye Cumhuriyet Merkez Bankasi **www.tcmb.gov.tr**
Uganda: Bank of Uganda **www.bou.or.ug**

Ukraine: National Bank of Ukraine **www.bank.gov.ua**
United Arab Emirates: Central Bank of the United Arab Emirates **www.cbuae.gov.ae**
United Kingdom: Bank of England **www.bankofengland.co.uk**
United States Federal Reserve System **www.federalreserve.gov/otherfrb.htm**
Uruguay: Banco Central del Uruguay **www.bcu.gub.uy**
Venezuela: Banco Central de Venezuela **www.bcv.org.ve**
West Africa: Banque Centrale des Etats de l'Afrique de l'Ouest **www.bceao.int**
Yemen: Central Bank of Yemen **www.centralbank.gov.ye**
Zimbabwe: Reserve Bank of Zimbabwe **www.rbz.co.zw**

APPENDIX F: BALANCE OF TRADE 2006

The following table shows exports, imports, and trade balance by country and area in millions of dollars as reported by the U.S. Census Bureau for November 2006. The data is not seasonally adjusted.

Details may not equal totals because of rounding. (X) Not applicable. (-) Represents zero or less than one-half unit of value shown.	November 2006		
Country	**Trade balance**	**Exports**	**Imports**
TOTAL SSS*	**-65,476.4**	**91,239.8**	**156,716.2**
Afghanistan	43.4	46.2	2.8
Albania	1.5	2.1	0.6
Algeria	-680.5	115.1	795.6
Andorra	-0.7	0.6	1.4
Angola	-455.7	313.4	769.1
Anguilla	3.4	3.5	0.1
Antigua and Barbuda	13.6	14.1	0.4
Argentina	50.9	402.8	351.9
Armenia	1.0	5.2	4.2
Aruba	-167.9	52.8	220.8
Australia	772.1	1,552.1	780.0
Austria	-555.6	261.2	816.9
Azerbaijan	-124.8	18.7	143.5

Bahamas	148.1	191.8	43.7
Bahrain	-0.7	43.4	44.0
Bangladesh	-216.6	30.0	246.7
Barbados	46.3	49.1	2.7
Belarus	-14.0	5.7	19.7
Belgium	908.3	1,961.2	1,052.9
Belize	9.4	18.0	8.6
Benin	11.1	11.1	(-)
Bermuda	36.7	38.3	1.7
Bhutan	-0.1	(-)	0.1
Bolivia	-9.8	20.6	30.5
Bosnia-Herzegovina	0.2	1.9	1.7
Botswana	-11.4	2.6	14.1
Brazil	-421.7	1,873.8	2,295.6
British Indian Ocean Territories	(-)	(-)	(-)
British Virgin Islands	5.3	12.6	7.3
Brunei	-29.8	2.8	32.6
Bulgaria	-12.4	19.1	31.5
Burkina	1.3	1.3	(-)
Burma (Myanmar)	0.5	0.5	(-)
Burundi	0.1	0.1	(-)
Cambodia	-185.1	6.3	191.4
Cameroon	-11.7	11.7	23.4
Canada	-5,417.9	19,480.7	24,898.7
Cape Verde	0.4	0.4	(-)
Cayman Islands	47.7	48.6	0.9

Central African Republic	5.3	5.5	0.2
Chad	-130.4	12.5	142.9
Chile	383.9	955.9	572.0
China	-22,918.8	4,858.3	27,777.1
Christmas Island	(-)	(-)	(-)
Cocos (Keeling) Island	-0.1	(-)	0.1
Colombia	21.5	620.4	598.9
Comoros	-0.3	(-)	0.3
Congo (Brazzaville)	-266.4	6.6	272.9
Congo (Kinshasa)	-0.7	11.5	12.2
Cook Islands	0.1	0.2	0.1
Costa Rica	26.8	359.0	332.2
Côte d'Ivoire	-19.8	11.5	31.4
Croatia	-31.8	9.1	40.9
Cuba	36.1	36.1	(-)
Cyprus	9.5	11.9	2.5
Czech Republic	-86.9	95.3	182.1
Denmark	-259.2	193.9	453.1
Djibouti	1.3	1.4	(-)
Dominica	5.2	5.5	0.2
Dominican Republic	136.4	501.5	365.0
East Timor	1.3	1.3	(-)
Ecuador	-248.9	276.9	525.9
Egypt	154.1	325.0	171.0
El Salvador	14.7	177.2	162.5
Equatorial Guinea	-23.4	23.8	47.2
Eritrea	0.1	0.3	0.1

Estonia	5.4	18.9	13.5
Ethiopia	2.3	6.8	4.5
Falkland Islands	-0.7	0.6	1.3
Faroe Islands	-0.4	0.2	0.6
Federal Republic of Germany	-4,122.6	3,566.6	7,689.2
Federated States of Micronesia	2.0	2.1	0.1
Fiji	-10.8	3.3	14.1
Finland	-162.3	250.6	412.9
France	-1,225.9	1,898.1	3,123.9
French Guiana	5.8	5.9	(-)
French Polynesia	4.6	8.2	3.7
French Southern and Antarctic Lands	(-)	(-)	(-)
Gabon	297.9	10.8	108.6
Gambia	1.5	1.5	(-)
Gaza Strip Administered by Israel	(-)	(-)	(-)
Georgia	3.4	24.2	20.8
Ghana	26.6	34.6	8.0
Gibraltar	15.5	15.6	(-)
Greece	98.5	176.5	78.0
Greenland	-1.1	0.1	1.2
Grenada	6.3	6.7	0.4
Guadeloupe	5.8	5.8	(-)

Guatemala	67.3	309.7	242.5
Guinea	1.3	6.6	5.2
Guinea-Bissau	-0.1	0.1	0.1
Guyana	9.9	16.7	6.8
Haiti	15.7	62.7	47.0
Heard and McDonald Islands	(-)	(-)	(-)
Honduras	-40.2	294.9	335.1
Hong Kong	917.7	1,544.2	626.6
Hungary	-91.6	102.6	194.3
Iceland	-0.8	17.7	18.6
India	-994.2	788.6	1,782.8
Indonesia	-828.9	247.6	1,076.5
Iran	-7.9	4.3	12.2
Iraq	-648.0	81.4	729.4
Ireland	-1,684.4	843.8	2,528.2
Israel	-726.9	990.7	1,717.6
Italy	-1,825.2	1,031.7	2,856.8
Jamaica	140.1	184.3	44.2
Japan	-7,900.7	5,075.4	12,976.0
Jordan	-67.5	45.5	113.0
Kazakhstan	-59.6	50.4	110.0
Kenya	78.3	106.9	28.6
Kiribati	0.1	0.2	0.1
Korea, South	-1,191.0	2,635.4	3,826.5
Kuwait	-242.3	150.2	392.5
Kyrgyzstan	16.2	16.3	0.1

Laos	-0.1	0.4	0.5
Latvia	15.2	22.6	7.4
Lebanon	91.0	100.9	9.9
Lesotho	-33.2	(-)	33.2
Liberia	-4.5	7.0	11.6
Libya	-129.7	107.3	237.0
Liechtenstein	-20.2	1.0	21.1
Lithuania	46.2	55.9	9.7
Luxembourg	-8.0	35.5	43.5
Macao	-55.7	20.4	76.2
Macedonia (Skopje)	-0.6	2.0	2.6
Madagascar	-18.9	2.8	21.6
Malawi	-6.4	2.0	8.4
Malaysia	-1,914.3	1,034.0	2,948.4
Maldives	1.1	1.3	0.1
Mali	6.8	7.2	0.4
Malta	-23.3	11.2	34.5
Marshall Islands	1.5	2.2	0.7
Martinique	2.4	2.6	0.2
Mauritania	8.5	8.6	(-)
Mauritius	-11.0	2.7	13.8
Mayott	(-)	(-)	(-)
Mexico	-5,440.3	11,779.8	17,220.1
Moldova	-0.6	2.0	2.6
Monaco	-0.4	1.1	1.5
Mongolia	-3.6	1.9	5.4
Montserrat	0.1	0.4	0.2

Morocco	17.2	49.6	32.4
Mozambique	3.8	3.8	(-)
Namibia	-7.5	8.2	15.7
Nauru	0.2	0.2	(-)
Nepal	-6.1	1.1	7.2
Netherlands	1,470.1	2,823.3	1,353.2
Netherlands Antilles	71.1	152.2	81.1
New Caledonia	0.1	7.2	7.1
New Zealand	-24.2	195.0	219.2
Nicaragua	-41.4	78.8	120.2
Niger	3.3	3.4	0.1
Nigeria	-1,682.0	200.7	1,882.6
Niue	1.8	1.8	(-)
Norfolk Island	0.2	0.2	(-)
North Korea	(-)	(-)	(-)
Norway	-255.8	217.0	472.7
Oman	52.8	64.3	11.5
Pakistan	-156.2	128.8	285.0
Palau	0.6	0.6	(-)
Panama	177.5	208.6	31.1
Papua New Guinea	-4.9	3.2	8.1
Paraguay	75.6	84.2	8.6
Peru	-189.3	314.6	503.9
Philippines	-113.9	651.9	765.8
Pitcairn Island	0.1	0.1	(-)
Poland	-23.2	160.5	183.7
Portugal	-148.5	151.9	300.4

Qatar	95.1	118.4	23.2
Republic of Yemen	-3.0	26.1	29.0
Reunion	0.4	1.0	0.6
Romania	-32.9	51.2	84.0
Russia	-612.0	446.6	1,058.7
Rwanda	-1.1	0.4	1.5
San Marino	0.1	0.2	0.1
Sao Tome and Principe	0.2	0.2	(-)
Saudi Arabia	-1,795.6	621.8	2,417.4
Senegal	3.9	12.0	8.1
Serbia and Montenegro	6.7	12.6	5.9
Seychelles	0.7	1.4	0.8
Sierra Leone	1.8	5.6	3.8
Singapore	963.0	2,464.8	1,501.8
Slovakia	-171.4	18.6	190.0
Slovenia	-25.9	22.7	48.7
Solomon Islands	0.5	0.7	0.1
Somalia	0.4	0.4	(-)
South Africa	-190.6	365.0	555.6
Spain	-139.8	732.1	871.9
Sri Lanka	-148.0	15.2	163.2
St Helena	0.1	0.1	0.1
St Kitts and Nevis	3.8	8.3	4.5
St Lucia	18.8	19.9	1.1
St Pierre and Miquelon	-0.1	(-)	0.1
St Vincent and the Grenadines	5.4	5.6	0.1

Sudan	11.8	12.3	0.5
Suriname	13.3	21.8	8.5
Svalbard, Jan Mayen Island	0.2	0.2	(-)
Swaziland	-10.4	0.6	10.9
Sweden	-791.5	363.5	1,155.0
Switzerland	4.7	1,320.0	1,315.3
Syria	14.2	39.5	25.3
Taiwan	-1,111.5	2,097.0	3,208.5
Tajikistan	9.4	9.4	(-)
Tanzania	3.1	6.9	3.7
Thailand	-707.3	1,336.1	2,043.5
Togo	5.6	5.6	(-)
Tokelau	1.4	1.8	0.4
Tonga	0.4	0.9	0.5
Trinidad and Tobago	-485.7	143.3	629.0
Tunisia	-6.5	46.7	53.3
Turkey	22.4	461.6	439.2
Turkmenistan	15.6	17.4	1.8
Turks and Caicos Islands	31.2	32.3	1.1
Tuvalu	(-)	(-)	(-)
Uganda	4.3	5.1	0.7
Ukraine	-66.8	60.9	127.7
United Arab Emirates	730.7	820.7	90.0
United Kingdom	-711.6	3,874.7	4,586.3
Uruguay	13.2	50.8	37.6

Uzbekistan	-54.2	3.5	57.7
Vanuatu	0.4	0.5	0.1
Vatican City	2.8	2.9	(-)
Venezuela	-1,638.3	909.8	2,548.1
Vietnam	-612.1	105.8	717.9
Wallis and Futuna	(-)	0.1	(-)
West Bank Administered by Israel	-0.1	0.1	0.2
Western Sahara	(-)	(-)	(-)
Western Samoa	1.0	1.3	0.2
Zambia	4.0	5.7	1.7
Zimbabwe	0.7	3.4	2.7
Unidentified (1)	37.2	37.2	(-)

U.S. Trade with the World
(seasonally adjusted)

NOTE: All figures are in millions of U.S. dollars.

Month	Exports	Imports	Balance
January 2006	82,247.0	153,227.0	-70,980.0
February 2006	81,662.0	148,449.0	-66,787.0
March 2006	83,265.0	149,682.0	-66,417.0
April 2006	82,768.0	151,035.0	-68,267.0
May 2006	85,109.0	154,718.0	-69,609.0
June 2006	87,908.0	156,586.0	-68,678.0
July 2006	86,547.2	158,515.8	-71,968.6
August 2006	89,240.0	162,454.0	-73,214.0
September 2006	89,885.0	1,585,460.0	-1,495,575.0
October 2006	89,805.0	153,416.0	-63,611.0
November 2006	90,700.0	153,496.0	-62,796.0
TOTAL	949,136.2	3,127,038.8	-2,177,902.6

- "TOTAL" may not add because of rounding.

- Table reflects only those months for which there was trade.

- CONTACT: Data Dissemination Branch, U.S. Census Bureau 301-763-2311

- SOURCE: U.S. Census Bureau, Foreign Trade Division, Data Dissemination Branch, Washington DC 20233

APPENDIX G: ECONOMIC INDICATORS FOR MAJOR TRADING MARKETS

	U.S. (dollar)	Europe (euro)	Japan (yen)	Great Britain (pound)	Switzerland (franc)	Canada (dollar)	Australia (dollar)	New Zealand[1] (dollar)
Major Trading Markets								
Type of Economy	Service-Oriented	Trade, Capital Flow & Service Oriented	Manufacture-Oriented	Service-Oriented	Capital and Trade Flows	Service-Oriented	Service-Oriented	Trade-Oriented
Central Bank	Federal Reserve Bank (Fed)	European Central Bank (ECB)	Bank of Japan (BOJ)	Bank of England (BOE)	Swiss National Bank (SNB)	Bank of Canada (BOC)	Reserve Bank of Australia (RBA)	Reserve Bank of New Zealand (RBNZ)
Central Bank Interest	Federal Funds Target Rate	ECB Minimum Bid Rate		Bank Repo Rate	Swiss LIBOR rate	Bank Rate	Cash Rate	

IMF estimate of GDP2		$12.2 trillion	$12.4 trillion	$3.9 trillion	$1.8 trillion	$236.9 million	$1.1 trillion	$630.1 million	$101.6 million
Inflation Target		Federal Funds Target Rate	0% to 2% of the HICP	0	2.5% growth in RPI-X3	Swiss Libor Rate	1%-3%	2%-3% of CPI	1.5% of CPI
Important Indicators									
Gross Domestic Product Ranking4		1st	Unranked	3rd	6th	39th	11th	17th	58th
Producer Price Index	PPI	X					X	X	X
Consumer Price Index	CPI	X	HICP			X	X	X	X
Industrial Production	IP	X	X	X	X	Production Index			
Institute Supply Management Index	ISM index	X							

Gross Domestic Product Ranking4		1st	Unranked	3rd	6th	39th	11th	17th	58th
Durable Goods and Services		X						Balance of Goods and Services	Balance of Goods and Services
Consumer Confidence		X							
Employment Cost Index	ECI	X	X	Data, not an Index	Data, not an Index		Data, not an Index		
Retail Sales	RSI	X			Retail Price Index	X			
Housing Starts		X			X				
Balance of International Trade		X					X		
Balance of Payments		X		X		X			

273

							Consumer Consumption	X
Private Consumption		X					X	
Treasury International Capital Flow	TIC flow							
Information and Forschung Survey	IFS		X					
Tankan Survey				X				
Budget Deficit			X					
Purchasing Manager's Index	PMI					X		
KoF					X			

1 Not a major currency, but the minor currency that trades the most volume.

2 Estimates of GDP as published in 2006 by the International Monetary Fund (IMF) with estimates for the year 2005.

3 RPI-X is the U.K. calculation of Retail price Index that excludes mortgage payments.

4 Rankings as published by the IMF for the year 2005

ABOUT THE AUTHOR

Jamaine Burrell is a freelance writer who lives in Baltimore. Her many talents have led to authorship of this book as well as other books under the Atlantic Publishing Group including "*The Rental Propery Manager's Toolbox — A Complete Guide Including Pre-Written Forms, Agreements, Letters, and Legal Notices: WIth Companion CD-ROM*" and "*How to Repair Your Credit Score Now — Simple No Cost Methods You Can Put to Uses Today.*"

KEY TO ABBREVIATIONS

ADX – average directional index
ASEAN – Association of Southeast Asian Nations
ASIC – Australian Securities and Investment Commission
AUD – Australian dollar

BEA – U.S. Bureau of Economic Analysis
BIS – Bank for International Settlements
BOC – Bank of Canada
BOE – Bank of England
BOJ – Bank of Japan
BoP – balance of payments
BRR – Brazilian real

CFTC – Commodity Futures Trading Commission
CME – Chicago Mercantile Exchange
CNY – Chinese yuan
CPI – Consumer Price Index
CTA – Commodity Trading Advisor

EBS – Electronic Broking System
ECB – European Central Bank
ECI – U.S. Employment Cost Index

EMU – European Monetary Union
ERM – exchange-rate mechanism
ESCB – European System of Central Banks
EUR – euro

FCMs – Futures Commission Merchants
Fed – U.S. Federal Reserve
FLO – Federal Labor Office
FOMC – Federal Open Market Committee
Forex – Foreign Exchange Market
FRB – Federal Reserve Board
FSA – Financial Service Authority of the United Kingdom

G8 – Group of Eight
GBP – British pound
GDP – gross domestic product
GDP – Gross Domestic Product

HICP – Harmonized Index of Consumer Prices
HSBC – Hong Kong and Shanghai Banking Corporation

IDAC – Investment Dealers Association of Canada
IMF – International Monetary Fund
IMM – International Monetary Market
IP – Industrial Production
ISM – Institute for Supply Management Index

KoF – Konjunkturforschungsstelle der eth, Zurich
KRW – South Korean won

LIBOR – London Interbank Offered Rates
LVTS – Canadian Large Value Transfer System

M&A – Merger and acquisition

M3 – measure of money supply

MOF – Japan's Ministry of Finance

MPC – Monetary Policy Committee

MUIP – Monetary Union Index of Consumer Prices

NASDAQ – National Association of Securities Dealers Automatic Quotation System

NFA – National Futures Association

NSA – non-seasonally adjusted

NYSE – New York Stock Exchange

NZD – New Zealand dollar

NZS – New Zealand superannuation

OCO – Order Cancels Others

OCR – official cash rate

OHLC – open/high/low/close

P/L – profit and loss

PIPs – Price Interest Points

PMI – Purchasing Manager's Index

PPI – Producer Price Index

PPP – Purchasing Power Parity

RBA – Reserve Bank of Australia

RBNZ – Reserve Bank of New Zealand

RPI – Retail Price Index

RSI – Retail Sales Index

SA – seasonally adjusted

SEC – Securities and Exchange Commission

SFBC – Swiss Federal Banking Commission

SFC – Securities and Futures Commission of Hong Kong

SGD – Singapore dollar

SMA – simple moving average

SNB – Swiss National Bank

STP – straight-through processing

USD – U.S. dollars

USDX – U.S. Dollar Index

ZAR – South African rand

INDEX

WALL STREET LINGO: THOUSANDS OF INVESTMENT TERMS EXPLAINED SIMPLY

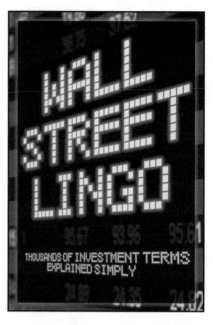

Wall Street Lingo is an essential reference that translates the jargon used on Wall Street into direct, easy to understand, Main Street language and organizes it the way you use it.

Finally, a finance dictionary compiled with the individual investor in mind. Wall Street Lingo does more than define the terms your stockbroker, the Wall Street Journal, and CNBC pitch at you. This book explains over 1,000 terms in a way that traditional dictionaries can't.

Where other dictionaries start at A and end at Z, Wall Street Lingo is organized in chapters, by subject. It begins where you begin, with a topic that has piqued your curiosity, and ends only when your curiosity has been satisfied. Here are some examples of topics covered:

Have you ever wondered about the difference between CPI and PPI? In other dictionaries, you'll find the definitions 200 pages apart. Wall Street Lingo brings them together in the chapter Economics for Investors.

If you think technical analysis is only for the pros, flip to the chapter Technically Speaking for dozens of plain English translations to stock chart terms like Bollinger bands, MACD, Elliott wave theory, and Bearish Divergence. It might change your mind.

Whether you're an experienced investor or are exploring the market for the first time, you'll appreciate the easy-reading style and unique structure of this innovative investment tool.

Also Available In Spanish!

ISBN-10: 1-60138-038-0 • ISBN-13: 978-1-60138-038-8
288 Pages • Item # WST-01 • $24.95

To order call 1-800-814-1132 or visit www.atlantic-pub.com

THE COMPLETE GUIDE TO INVESTING IN REAL ESTATE TAX LIENS & DEEDS: HOW TO EARN HIGH RATES OF RETURN — SAFELY

THE COMPLETE GUIDE TO

Investing in Real Estate Tax Liens & Deeds

HOW TO EARN HIGH

RATES OF RETURN —

SAFELY

Purchasing tax liens instruments from city, county and municipal governments can provide you with very high and very secure rates of return in some cases as high as 12%, 18%, 24% or even 1,000% or more per year. If performed correctly, investments in tax lien instruments will far out pace stock market performance, even traditional real estate investments. The key is to know how to perform this process correctly.

Tax lien certificates and deeds are not purchased thru a broker. You purchase these property tax liens directly from the state or county government (depending on the state). This type of investment was created by state law, and state law protects you as the investor. Individuals investing in tax liens and deeds can be very rewarding. Tax liens can be tax deferred or even tax free. You can purchase them in your self-directed IRA. Interest rates vary but average between 4% and 18%. The interest rates are fixed, by local governments, essentially a government guaranteed loan. Additionally the investment is secured by real property (real estate).

So this sounds great what is the catch? There really is none except you must know what you are doing! This ground breaking and exhaustively researched new book will provide everything you need to know to get you started on generating high investment returns with low risk from start to finish. You will learn: What property tax liens and tax lien certificates are, how to invest in tax lien certificates, How to buy tax lien certificates, Insider secrets to help you double or even triple your investment, how to start with under $1,000.00 dollars, The risks, traps and pitfalls to avoid, and a detailed directory of states that sell tax lien certificates with contact information.

ISBN-10: 0-910627-73-8 • ISBN-13: 978-0-910627-73-3
320 Pages • Item #CGI-02 • $21.95

To order call 1-800-814-1132 or visit www.atlantic-pub.com

DID YOU BORROW THIS COPY?

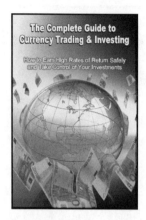